Ruf
Nachts flogen die Gomuli

By night the gomuls
took to the skies
to hunt

Ночью гомулы
поднялись на небо
чтобы охотиться

Nachts flogen die Gomuli
in den Himmel,
um zu jagen

Nachts flogen die Gomuli

Eine Anthologie mit Gedichten über Georg Wilhelm Steller, Vitus Jonassen Bering und Kamtschatka

Herausgegeben
von
Joachim Ruf

3. Auflage

Norderstedt, Books on Demand
2019

Umschlag

„Gomuli" sind nach G.W. Steller monströse Fabelwesen auf Kamtschatka, das hier mit seinen Vulkanen und mit den weiteren Elementen der Anthologie, der Steller-schen Seekuh und der Beringinsel, als Kartenskizze von Sven Waxell, 1742 dargestellt ist.

© 2019 Joachim Ruf, Mühltal
Gestaltung von Textkörper, Abbildungen und
Umschlag: Harald Pinl, Celle

Herstellung und Verlag:
BoD – Books on Demand, Norderstedt

ISBN: 9783735737175

Inhalt

Gedichte über Kamtschatka
und die Kommandeur-Inseln

Nachwort: Alexander Puschkin über
Kamtschatka, Krascheninnikow und Steller

Vorwort

Auf der Website der Steller-Gesellschaft sind zwei Bände von W.G. Sebald und Andrej Bronnikov aufgeführt, in denen Gedichte über Georg Wilhelm Steller enthalten sind. Steller hatte als Arzt und Naturforscher von 1737 bis 1743 an der Zweiten russischen Kamtschatka-Expedition unter dem Kapitän Vitus Jonassen Bering teilgenommen. Inzwischen habe ich eine Fülle von Gedichten über Georg Steller, die Stellersche Seekuh, den Stellerschen Häher (Schwarzkopf- oder Diademhäher), Vitus Bering und Kamtschatka zusammengetragen, die es wert sind, in einer Anthologie veröffentlicht zu werden. Margritt Engel machte mich mit Gedichten über Steller's Sea Cow und Steller's Jay von Robert Hass und Tom Sexton bekannt.

Das Gedicht von Eleni Sikelianos „Steller's Sea Cow" hat mich besonders berührt und vor allem die erste Zeile: „By night the gomuls took to the skies to hunt". Die Faszination der ersten Zeile dieses Gedichtes hat zum Titel dieser Anthologie geführt: „Nachts flogen die Gomuli".

Mit den „Gomuli", russisch камули/kamuli, hatte Steller als Erster die gottähnlichen, gigantischen Wesen beschrieben, die Monstern ähneln und in den Sagen der Kamtschadalen auftreten. In knappen Worten fasst Sikelianos das Geschehen der letzten Tage auf der später so genannten Bering-Insel vor Kamtschatka zusammen: Bering erreicht mit seinem Schiff diese Insel, stirbt und ein Teil der Mannschaft kann sich durch den Verzehr des wohlschmeckenden Fleisches der Seekühe ernähren und überleben.

Die Steller'sche Seekuh

Steller war der einzige Naturforscher, der jemals eine

9

lebendige Seekuh gesehen hatte, bevor sie 1768, nur 27 Jahre nach ihrer Entdeckung, von Robben- bzw. Pelztierjägern ausgerottet wurde. Steller erkannte, dass die Seekuh mit den Manatis aus dem Atlantik verwandt war, die Georg Marcgraf, ein aus Liebstadt bei Pirna stammender Naturforscher, in Historia Naturalis Brasiliae mit Willem Piso erstmalig 1648 beschrieb. Aber auch der Weltumsegler und Entdecker William Dampier beschrieb 1697 die Manatis. Die Steller'sche Seekuh war die einzige Vegetarierin unter diesen Säugetieren und Steller beschrieb vier Arten von Seetang, die sie aß. Wegen ihrer rindenartigen Haut wurden die Stellerschen Seekühe früher auch „Borkentiere" genannt.

Der lateinische Name für die Seekuh, sirenia, weist darauf hin, dass Erzählungen nach einsame Seeleute Seekühe (oder Manatis) für Sirenen hielten, für weibliche Fabelwesen, die durch ihren betörenden Gesang Schiffer anlockten, um sie zu töten.

Neben den oben genannten Schriften von Sebald und Bronnikov liegen noch andere umfangreichere Gedichtswerke zum Thema dieser Schrift vor, wie z.B. „Eastward Ho! – The Saga of Vitus Bering" von Jennifer Dunbar Dorn. Aus ihnen werden daher nur einzelne Gedichte exemplarisch wiedergegeben.

Bemerkenswert erscheint, dass sich mehrere der Steller-Gedichte, besonders im amerikanischen Raum, mit der Ausrottung der Stellerschen Seekuh beschäftigen. So die Gedichte von Davie, Day, Fama, Lewis, Macari, Sexton und Zuzga. Es wird als ein frühes Beispiel für das negative Eingreifen des Menschen in natürliche Lebensräume gesehen, das sich nicht mehr rückgängig machen lässt. Auch im deutschen Sprachraum ist die Ausrottung in der Lyrik zum Thema geworden. So in Heinrich Deterings „Requiem für eine Seekuh" oder Mikael Vogels Gedichtband „Dodos auf der Flucht – Requiem für ein verlorenes Bestiarium", in dem Steller zitiert und auf die Zerstörung unserer Umwelt hingewiesen wird.

Poesie kann als generelle Bereicherung und Ergänzung zur Naturwissenschaft gesehen werden. Poesie kann wissenschaftliche Prozesse bereichern und andere neue Zugänge ermöglichen. Insofern wird auch diese Gedichtanthologie zu Steller, Bering und Kamtschatka die Stellerforschung durch Verdichtung und Erweiterung bereichern können.

Dank

Diese Anthologie wäre nicht ohne die Hinweise auf Gedichte von Frau Prof. em. Dr. Margritt Engel, Anchorage, Elisabeth Hintzsche, Ullrich Wannhoff und vielen anderen zustandegekommen. Mein Dank gilt ihnen und den Autorinnen und Autoren der Gedichte, die mir bereitwillig Auskünfte über ihre Gedichte, deren Entstehung und über die Bücher, in denen die Gedichte abgedruckt wurden, gaben. Freundlicherweise haben sie mir auch ihre Abdruckgenehmigung gegeben. Mit einigen Autoren stehe ich heute noch in Verbindung. Mein ganz besonderer Dank gilt dem Historiker für Russische und Umwelt-Geschichte Dr. Harald Pinl, der die Gestaltung dieser Anthologie übernommen hat.

In welchen Werken und wo (Verlag, Internetplattform) die einzelnen Gedichte erschienen sind, wird im Quellenverzeichnis angegeben. Die Herkunft der Abbildungen wird am Schluss des Buches in einem eigenen Verzeichnis nachgewiesen.

Mühltal, im Oktober 2019   Joachim Ruf

Gedichte über
Georg Wilhelm Steller

Steller-Skulptur von Il'ja V'juev, 2009

STELLERS LEBENSLAUF
von W. G. Sebald

I

Der aus Windsheim in Franken
gebürtige Georg Wilhelm Steller
stieß im Verlauf seines Studiums
an der Universität Halle wiederholt
auf die in die Intelligenzblätter eingerückte
Nachricht,
daß die russische Zarin Anstalten treffe,
im Zuge der Erweiterung ihres Reichs
eine Expedition von noch nie dagewesenem
Ausmaß
unter dem Oberkommando des Vitus Bering,
dessen Kopf zirka zweieinhalb Jahrhunderte später
zu unserem Entsetzen noch einmal
in der Literatur auftaucht,
an die pazifischen Küsten zu entsenden,
damit von dort aus der Seeweg
nach Amerika in Erfahrung gebracht werde.

III

Obschon es hieß, daß ihn die Obrigkeit
in kürzester Frist auf den Lehrstuhl
für Botanik berufen und somit
in der bürgerlichen Societät

akkreditieren werde, ging Steller,
mittellos, wie er war, und kaum
mehr als seine Notizbücher in der Tasche,
bereits an dem auf das Rigorosum
folgenden Tag mit der Post
nach der von russischen Truppen
belagerten Stadt Danzig,
wo er sich als medizinischer Assistent
auf einem Packboot anheuern ließ,
das einige hundert Invalide
nach Rußland zurückbringen sollte.

VIII

Als Steller 1736 tatsächlich
den ersehnten Auftrag erhielt,
der Beringschen Expedition sich anzuschließen,
war dieses bereits zehn Jahre zuvor
in die Wege geleitete Unternehmen,
das aus einem Heer von Zimmermännern,
Schmieden, Fuhrknechten, Seeleuten,
Schreibern, kommandierenden
Chargen, Wissenschaftlern
und Assistenten bestand
und nicht nur Baumaterial, Werkzeug, Instrumente,
ein Arsenal von Waffen und Aberhunderte
von Büchern, sondern auch endlose
Fouragierzüge, zur Verpflegung der Mannschaft,

Geschirr und Garderobe und kistenweise
Bordeauxwein für die höher gestellten
Envoyés der Akademie vorwärtszubringen hatte,
nicht anders als ein schwere Geröllmassen
mit sich fortbewegender Gletscher,
in Jakutsk auf dem einhundertneunundzwanzigsten
Grad östlicher Länge angelangt.

X

Am 20. März des Jahres 1741
betritt Steller das langgestreckte
Blockhaus der Kommandantur von Petropawlowsk
an der Ostküste der Halbinsel Kamtschatka.
In einem fensterlosen, nicht mehr als
sechs mal sechs Fuß messenden
Verschlag am hinteren Ende
des sonst auf keine Weise unterteilten
Innenraums dieses Gebäudes
findet er Bering, den Kommandeur-Kapitän,
an einem aus Planken zusammengenagelten,
von weißfleckigen Land- und Seekarten
über und über bedeckten Tisch,
den neunundfünfzigjährigen
Kopf in die Fläche der rechten,
mit einem Flügelpaar
tätowierten Hand gestützt,
einen Stechzirkel in der Linken,

bewegungslos sitzen
bei einem blakenden Licht.
Es braucht eine unheimlich
lange Zeit, denkt Steller,
bis Bering die Augen
aufmacht und hinschaut
zu ihm. Ein Tier
ist der Mensch, in tiefe
Trauer gehüllt,
in einen schwarzen Mantel,
mit schwarzem
Pelzwerk
gefüttert.

XIII

Bei Anbruch des folgenden Tags,
dem Namensfest des hl. Elias,
ging Steller an Land. Zehn Stunden
hatte ihm Bering, dem das Grauen
bereits an die Stirn geschrieben war,
zugestanden für eine wissenschaftliche Exkursion.
Von einer tiefgründigen Bläue
war jetzt das Wasser und waren die Wälder,
die herabwuchsen bis an die Küste
des Meers. Unverstört näherten sich
Steller die Tiere, schwarze und rote
Füchse, auch Elstern, Häher und Krähen

gingen mit ihm auf dem Weg
über den Strand. Im durchsichtigen Dunkel
zwischen den Bäumen bewegte er sich
mit geradezu schwebendem Schritt
über die einen Fuß dicken Polster aus Moos.
Nahe war er daran, bergwärts
immer nur weiterzugehen, hinein
in die kühle Wildnis, aber die Konstruktionen
der Wissenschaft in seinem Kopf,
ausgerichtet auf eine Verringerung
der Unordnung in der Welt,
widersetzten sich diesem Bedürfnis.

Später in einer aus Fichtenstämmen
zusammengefügten Behausung erlebt er
die Wirkung verlassener Dinge
in einem fremden Raum. Ein kreisrundes
Trinkgefäß aus geschälter Rinde,
einen mit Kupfererz durchsprenkelten
Wetzstein, ein fischköpfiges Paddel
und eine Kinderrassel aus gebranntem Ton
sucht er mit Vorsicht sich aus und hinterlegt
statt dessen einen eisernen Kessel, eine Schnur
mit bunt aneinandergereihten Perlen,
ein Fetzchen bucharische Seide,
ein halbes Pfund Tabak und
eine chinesische Pfeife.
An diesen schweigsamen Handel

erinnert sich noch nach einem halben Jahrhundert,
wie aus einem Bericht des Commandeurs Billings
hervorgeht,
einer der Bewohner dieser abgesonderten Gegend
mit einem raschelnd nach innen
gekehrten Lachen.

XVII

Sechs Jahre dauerte es,
bis die Überlebenden der Expedition
Order erhielten,
in die Hauptstadt zurückzukommen.
Steller aber hatte sich wenige Tage
nach Ankunft in der Bucht von Avatscha
vom Korps abgesetzt und war mit dem Kosacken
Lepekhin
zu Fuß ins Innere der Halbinsel aufgebrochen.
Wenn Dir die Reise gefällig ist,
sei unser Antrieb beim Gehen,
sprach er bei sich, sei
Trost auf dem Weg, Schatten
im Schwülen des Mittags,
Licht in der Finsternis,
Decke wider Frost und Regen,
Wagen in der Stunde der Müdigkeit,
Hilfe in der Noth, auf daß wir,
unter Deiner Führung, fahrlos dort eintreffen,

wo es uns hinzieht;
trag Du die Sorge, Herr,
damit die Sterne günstig
über uns sich scharen.

XVIII

Den übrigen Teil des Sommers
sammelt Steller botanisches Material,
füllt getrocknete Samen in Tütchen,
beschreibt, rubriziert, zeichnet,
in seinem schwarzen Reisezelt sitzend,
zum erstenmal glücklich in seinem Leben.
Thoma Lepekhin fängt Lachs,
bringt Pilze, Beeren und Blätter,
macht Feuer und Tee.
Den Winter hindurch
unterrichtet der deutsche Doktor
Koryackenkinder in einer winzigen,
hölzernen Schule, schreibt, als das Eis bricht,
Memoranda zur Verteidigung
der von der Marinekommandantur in Bolscheretsk
malträtierten und in ihrem Recht verkürzten
eingeborenen Stämme, was dazu führt,
daß ein Brief gegen ihn ausgestellt wird,
daß Verhöre stattfinden,
daß sich Mißverständnisse ergeben,
daß Verhaftungen erfolgen und daß Steller

jetzt vollends den Unterschied begreift
zwischen Natur und Gesellschaft.
Westwärts, Strecke um Strecke legt er
fliehend zurück, und es scheint ihm,
als gehe nun alles bergab.
Erst in Tara erreicht ihn die Nachricht,
er könne auf jedem beliebigen Weg
aufbrechen in seine Heimat.
Steller mietet drei Pferde,
fährt nach Tobolsk
und trinkt dort, er, der nie trank,
ganze drei Tage.
Danach kommt das Fieber,
er kriecht in den Schlitten,
heißt den Tataren weiterfahren nach Süden,
die einhundertsiebzig Meilen bis Tyumen.
Das ist infirmitas, die Brechung
der Zeit von Tag zu Tag
und von Stunde zu Stund,
der Rost und das Feuer
und das Salz der Planeten,
die Dunkelheit unter Tags
noch die Lichter am Himmel.

XIX

Manuskripte am Ende des Lebens,
geschrieben auf einer Insel im Eismeer,

mit kratzendem Gänsekiel und galliger Tinte,
Verzeichnisse von zweihundertelf
verschiedenen Pflanzen,
Geschichten von weißen Raben,
seltsamen Kormoranen und Seekühen,
eingebracht in den Staub
einer endlosen Registratur,
sein zoologisches Meisterwerk,
de bestiis marinis,
Reiseprogramm für die Jäger,
Leitfaden beim Zählen der Pelze,
nein, nicht hoch genug
war der Norden.

XX

In Tyumen holen sie ihn aus dem Schlitten,
schleppen sie seinen zur Hälfte versteinerten Leib
aus dem Eis hinein in das Feuer,
in ein waberndes Haus.
Jetzt fängt Alchimia an,
erkennt Steller den mortem improvisam,
den Schlag und all sein Anhang,
sieht seinen Tod, wie er sich spiegelt,
im Einglas des Feldscher.
Also seid ihr doctores,
verschüttete Lampen,
also prozediert die Natur

mit einem gottlosen
Lutheraner aus Deutschland.

XXI

Pallas berichtet, wie sie Steller,
den er verehrte, anderen Tages,
in seinen roten Umhang gehüllt,
ein gutes Stück außerhalb der Raststatt
der Rechtgläubigen in einen engen Graben
hoch über dem Ufer der Tura legten
und einen Hügel aufwarfen
von gefrorenen Wasen.
Auch schreibt Pallas, daß der Tote
noch träumte von den grasenden
Mammuts jenseits des Flusses,
bis in der Nacht einer kam
und seinen Mantel sich holte
und ihn liegen ließ im Schnee
wie einen erschlagenen Fuchs.

„Nach der Natur", 1995
Auswahl aus Gedichten I – XXI

Stellers
Handschrift:
Schluss eines
Ersuchens aus
Krasnoe Selo bei
Solikamsk an die
Akademie der
Wissenschaften in
Sankt Petersburg,
vom 18.08.1746

23

GMELIN ON STELLER
by Jennifer Dunbar Dorn

"He was not troubled about his clothing;
he used no wig and no powder; any kind
of boot or shoe suited him. In Siberia
he reduced his housekeeping outfit
to the smallest compass.
His drinking cup for beer was the same as
his cup for mead and whisky.
Wine he dispensed with entirely.
He had only one dish out of which
he ate and in which was served all his food.
For this he needed no chef —
he cooked everything himself
and that with so little circumstance
that soup, vegetables and meat were put
into the same pot and boiled together.
Smoke and smell in the room
in which he worked did not affect him.
It was no hardship for him to go hungry
and thirsty a whole day
if he was able to accomplish something
advantageous to science."

„Eastward Ho!", 2015

STELLER ALS GELEHRTER
von Anonymos

Стеллер Георг – фанатичный учёный.

Флорой и фауной был увлечённый.

Он об Америке страстно мечтал,

За полчаса там гербарий собрал.

Труд написал о корове Морской,

Знает весь мир о

животном таком.

Он описал её и срисовал,

Имя своё он коровушке

дал.

„Stikhi", 2019

STELLER ALS GELEHRTER
von Anonymos, übersetzt von Joachim Ruf

Steller Georg – war ein fanatischer Wissenschaftler.

Von der Flora und Fauna war er begeistert.

Er träumte leidenschaftlich von Amerika.

In einer halben Stunde sammelte er dort Herbarien.

Er schrieb eine Abhandlung über die Seekuh.

Die ganze Welt kennt

solch ein Tier.

Er beschrieb und zeichnete es.

Seinen Namen gab er der Kuh.

THE MERMAIDS OF
BROBDINGNAG
by Richard George

It was every zoologist's dream.
In this fjord-Iceland
the other side of the New World,
Sirenians, sea cows
but narwhal-dwarfing, mountainous –
and here he was, Georg Steller,
administering baptism.
Through chilly April sunsets
where only the sky's yellow-ochre
spoke of Spring, he watched them mate,
feeling for the one hither-
thithered by his lover's
double-ballet, catch me, catch me not.
They even slept on their back. He thought:
„How little divides us".
But what do you eat, in Kamchatka?
How do you keep warm?

He went with the hunters.
The details tore his heart out:
the massive hook, the ropes,
the beating, and the desperate
devotion of the male
‚even when she was dead'

as he told the clean white page
(the fat burned without smoke).

In Europe, he petitioned.
Siberia's longitude
intervened. He fell
twenty years before his mermaid:
an Arctic mercy.

In 1962,
off Cape Navarin, far to the north,
a pod of black giants perplexed
a whaling ship. Science
helter-skeltered from Moscow.

You can't fast-net an echo.

„Poem Hunter", 2005

Blick auf die Reede von St. Peter und St. Paul. Motiv einer Philatelie-Postkarte zum 275. Geburtstag von Steller, 1984

WILHELM STELLER
by Robert Hass

Wilhelm Steller, form's
hero, made
a healing broth.

He sailed with Bering
and the crew despised him,
a mean impatient man

born low enough
to hate the lower class.
For two years

he'd connived to join
the expedition and put
his name to all the beasts
and flowers of the north.
Now Bering sick,
the crew half mad with scurvy,

no one would let him
go ashore. Panic,
the maps were useless,

the summer weather almost gone.
He said, there are herbs
that can cure you,

I can save you all. He didn't
give a damn about them
and they knew it. For two years

he'd prepared. Bering listened.
Asleep in his bunk, he'd
seen death writing in the log.

On the island while
the sailors searched for water
Steller gathered herbs

and looking up
he saw the blue, black-crested
bird, shrilling in a pine.

His mind flipped to
Berlin, the library, a glimpse
he'd had at Audubon,

a blue-gray crested bird
exactly like the one
that squawked at him, a

Carolina jay, unlike
any European bird; he knew
then where they were.
America, we're saved.
No one believed him, or
sick for home, he didn't care

what wilderness
it was. They set sail
west. Bering died.
Steller's jay, by which
I found Alaska.
He wrote it in his book.

*

Saved no one. Still,
walking in the redwoods
I hear the cry

thief, thief, and
think of **Wilhelm Steller**;
in my dream we

are all saved. Camping
on a clement shore
in early fall, a strange land.

We feast most delicately.
The swans are stuffed with grapes,
the turkey with walnut

and chestnut and wild plum.
The river is our music: **unalaska**
(to make bread from acorns

we leach the tannic acid out —
this music, child,
and more, much more!)

When I was just
your age, the war was over
and we moved.

An Okie family lived
next door to our new
country house. That summer

Quincy Phipps was saved.
The next his house became
an unofficial Pentecostal church.

Summer nights: hidden
in the garden I ate figs,
watched where the knobby limbs

rose up and flicked
against the windows where
they were. O Je – sus.

Kissed and put to bed,
I slipped from the window
to the eaves and nestled

by the loquat tree.
The fruit was yellow-brown
in daylight, under the moon

pale clusters hung
like other moons, O
Je – sus, and I picked them;

the fat juices
dribbling down my chin,
I sucked and listened.

Men groaned. The women
sobbed and moaned, a
long unsteady belly-deep

bewildering sound, half
pleasure and half pain
that ended sometimes

in a croon, a broken song;
O Je – sus,
Je – sus.

*

That is what I have
to give you, child, stories,
songs, loquat seeds,

curiously shaped; they
are the frailest stay against
our fears. Death

in the sweetness, in the bitter
and the sour, death
in the salt, your tears,

this summer ripe and overripe.
It is a taste in the mouth,
child. We are the song

death takes its own time
singing. It calls us
as I call you child

to calm myself. It is every
thing touched casually,
lovers, the images

of saviors, books, the coin
I carried in my pocket
till it shone, it is

all things lustered
by the steady thoughtlessness
of human use.

„Songs to Survive the Summer", 1979

WILHELM STELLER
von Robert Hass, übersetzt von Margritt Engel

Wilhelm Steller, ein Held
von Format, machte
eine heilsame Suppe.

Er segelte mit Bering
und die Besatzung verachtete ihn,
den unfreundlichen, ungeduldigen Mann,

der, selbst niedrig geboren,
die unteren Klassen hasste.
Zwei Jahre lang

hatte er's erduldet, um
der Expedition beizutreten und
all den Tieren und den Blumen

des Nordens seinen Namen anzuhängen.
Nun ist Bering krank,
die Besatzung halb verrückt vom Skorbut;

niemand wollte ihn an Land
gehen lassen. Panik,
die Karten waren nutzlos,

das Sommerwetter fast vorbei.
Er sagte, es gäbe Kräuter,
die sie heilen könnten:

ich kann euch alle retten. Doch sie kümmerten
ihn einen Dreck, und das wussten sie.
Zwei Jahre lang

hatte er sich vorbereitet. Bering hörte auf ihn.
Im Schlaf in seiner Koje hatte er
den Tod ins Logbuch schreiben sehen.

Auf der Insel, während die Seeleute
Wasser suchten, sammelte
Steller Kräuter

und bemerkte beim Aufsehen
den blauen, schwarzköpfigen
Vogel, der in einer Kiefer kreischte.

Seine Gedanken gingen nach
Berlin, der Bibliothek, einen kurzen Blick
hatte er in den „Audubon" geworfen,

ein blau-grauer Vogel mit Schopf
genau wie der,
der ihn hier ankreischte, ein

Carolina-Häher, anders als irgendein
europäischer Vogel; da wusste er,
wo sie waren:

in Amerika, wir sind gerettet.
Keiner glaubte ihm, oder war so
heimwehkrank, es war ihm egal,

welche Wildnis
das war. Sie segelten
nach Westen. Bering starb.

Stellers Häher, auf Grund dessen
ich Alaska fand.
Das schrieb er in sein Buch.

Keiner gerettet. Aber
auf dem Weg durch die Redwoods
hör ich den Schrei

Dieb, Dieb und
denk an Wilhelm Steller;
in meinem Traum werden

wir alle gerettet. Wir campen
an einem milden Strand,
im Frühherbst, in fremdem Land.

Das Essen ist köstlich,
die Schwäne mit Trauben gefüllt,
der Truthahn mit Walnuss

und Kastanie und wilden Pflaumen.
Der Fluss ist unsre Musik: Unalaska
(um Brot aus Eicheln zu machen

laugen wir die Tanninsäure aus ---
diese Musik, Kind,
und mehr, viel mehr!)

COSSACK SONG
by Doraine Bennett

Old Hesselberg, half dead,
mans the helm.
Scurvy is our master.
Waxell gives no orders.
Bering lies helpless on his bunk.
None listen to Herr Steller.
The ship drifts, deadwood in a tossing sea.

Never will I carry
Lena to the Cossack crug,
nor have their blessing
to call her wife,
will not raise sons
faithful to serve my tsar,
teach them the ways of war,
share their prayers at evensong.

A Cossack should die in battle,
not drowned in the sea.
What else to do but sing?

"Stormy clouds delirious straying,
Showers of whirling snowflakes white,
And the pallid moonbeams waning —
Sad the heavens, sad the night."

"Ditty of the Month Club", 2016

37

THE SECOND SUMMONS, 1741
by Doraine Bennett

Months ago, Bering turned Herrn Steller away.
Herr Steller argued that to gather plants
never seen by men, to discover
what strange birds and beasts
lived in that uncharted world was needed.
No one could perform it as he.

Bering's hand waved him off.
He had no orders for a botanist to sail
beyond Kamchatka. No orders to travel.

Herr Steller consoled himself with salmon,
recording their strange habit,
the surge upstream to spawn and die.
Gorbuscha, keta, nerka, kibutch —
humpback, chum, sockeye, and silver.
He gave them their names,
studied their ways, until
the second summons came.

Herr Steller hid his surprise
at Bering's slackened jaw,
sagging cheeks on a face
once round as the moon,
hair stark white, sea-blue eyes

staring at the pile of useless maps
drawn from rumor and guess.
His voice, an echo of the former man,
desired Herrn Steller sail with him,
be his physician, in case…

The half-spoken thought
stretched between them
like an uncharted ocean.

Herr Steller hid his eagerness
as the captain-commander hid his relief.
Bering's hand shook his doctor's hand.
He lay down on the cot.
Herr Steller closed the door, prepared to sail,
while the captain-commander's weary hand
wavered,
adrift, over sunken eyes.

„Global Explorers", 2011

**Sonderstempel
der Deutschen Post
zu Stellers
Geburtstag 1984**

DIE ZWEITE AUFFORDERUNG
von Doraine Bennett, übersetzt von Joachim Ruf

Vor Monaten hat Bering Herrn Steller abgewiesen.
Herr Steller argumentierte, Pflanzen zu sammeln
nie von Menschen gesehen, zu entdecken
Was an seltsamen Vögeln und Tieren
lebte in dieser unerforschten Welt, würde benötigt.
Niemand könnte es so machen wie er.

Berings Hand winkte ab.
Er hatte keinen Befehl, mit einem Botaniker
zu segeln
jenseits von Kamtschatka. Keine Befehle zu reisen.

Herr Steller tröstete sich mit Lachs,
ihre seltsame Gewohnheit aufzuzeichnen,
die Welle stromaufwärts, um zu laichen und zu
sterben.
Gorbuscha-, Keta-, Nerka-, Kibutch-Lachse,
Buckel-, Hunds-, Rot- und Silberlachse.
Er gab ihnen ihre Namen,
studierte ihre Lebensweise,
bis die zweite Aufforderung kam.

Herr Steller verbarg seine Überraschung
über Bering's gesunkenen Unterkiefer,
schlaffe Wangen im Gesicht,
das einst wie der Mond,
Haare stark weiß, meerblaue Augen

starrte auf den Haufen nutzloser Karten
gezeichnet nach Gerücht und Raten.
Seine Stimme, ein Echo des früheren Mannes,
wünscht, Herr Steller segle mit ihm
als sein Arzt, falls …

Der halb ausgesprochene Gedanke
zwischen ihnen gestreckt
wie ein unerforschter Ozean.

Herr Steller verbarg seinen Eifer
als der Kapitan-Komandor seine Erleichterung
verbarg.
Berings Hand schüttelte die Hand seines Arztes.
Er legte sich in die Koje.
Herr Steller schloss die Tür, bereit zu segeln,
während die müde Hand des
Kapitan-Komandors schwankte,
treibend, über eingesunkene Augen.

STRANDED : VOICE OF THOMAS LEPEKHIN
by Doraine Bennett

Desperate sailors crawl on deck
Strain to see this miserable spit of land,
dig up a hidden cache of brandy,
celebrate what must be Kamchatka.
It is not Kamchatka.

It's a damn island where foxes
draw back their lips and snarl,
charge and snap my legs.
I beat the creatures off with driftwood,
sticks dug from snow-covered sand.
Seabirds scream over crashing waves.

Herr Steller is the cause of this misfortune.
God will help, he tells me.
If you cannot wait on me,
I will wait on you.

Good enough. I will gladly serve you,
you who brought me to this misery.
Who compelled you to go with these people?
Could you not enjoy good times
home on the Bolshaya River?

We are both alive, he says:
If I have dragged you into this misery,
you have in me with God's help,
a lifelong friend, a benefactor.
My intentions were good, Thoma.
Let yours be good, also.

Besides, you do not know
what might have happened at home.
He gives comfort
like the croak of ravens on the beach.
And takes his own in the strange, giant
creatures that lie in the surf,
upturned like boats.

„Global Explorers", 2011

Wilhelm Georg Steller
Gemälde von D.P. Lopatin, 2016

GESTRANDET : DIE STIMME VON THOMAS LEPECHIN
von Doraine Bennett, übersetzt von Joachim Ruf

Verzweifelte Seeleute kriechen an Deck,
strengen sich an, diese elende Landzunge zu sehen,
einen versteckten Vorrat von Brandy auszugraben,
zu feiern, was Kamtschatka sein muss.
Es ist nicht Kamtschatka.

Es ist eine verdammte Insel, wo Füchse
die Zähne fletschen und knurren,
angreifen und nach meinen Beinen schnappen.
Ich schlug die Biester mit Treibholz weg.
Stöcke aus verschneitem Sand gegraben.
Seevögel schreien über stürzende Wellen.

Herr Steller ist die Ursache dieses Unglücks.
Gott wird helfen, sagt er mir.
Wenn du mich nicht bedienen kannst,
Ich werde dich bedienen.

Gut genug. Ich werde dir gerne dienen,
du, der mich in dieses Elend gebracht hat.
Wer hat dich dazu gezwungen, mit diesen Leuten
zu gehen?
Konntest du keine guten Zeiten genießen?
Zuhause am Bolshaya River?

Wir sind beide am Leben, sagt er …
Wenn ich dich in dieses Elend gezogen habe,
du hast in mir mit Gottes Hilfe,
einen lebenslangen Freund, einen Wohltäter.
Meine Absichten waren gut, Thomas.
Lass deine auch gut sein.

Außerdem weißt du nicht
was zu Hause passiert sein könnte.
Er gibt Trost
wie krächzende Raben am Strand.
Und findet selbst Trost in den seltsamen
riesigen Tieren, die wie umgekehrte Boote
in der Brandung liegen.

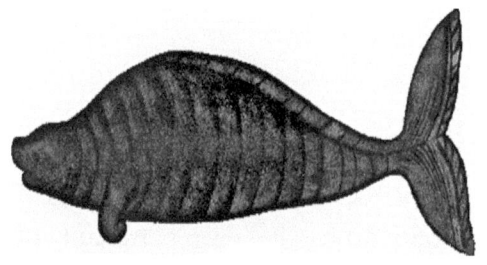

Stellersche Seekuh nach Sven Waxell, 1742

MURDER BALLAD
by Brian Barker

Georg Wilhelm Steller married his sea cow
in a simple ceremony on a Bering Island beach.
Five scurvied crewmen bore witness.
In lieu of rings, the couple exchanged garlands
of kelp
which the blushing bride quickly devoured.
That night, while she snored next to him,
the naturalist wrote in his journal:

She is insatiable! Her skin is black and thick,
gnarled like an ancient oak.
Toothless, the space between her lips is packed
with a dense array of thick brisles,
the kissing of which I dare not describe.
When her stunted flippers draw my head to her bosom,
I feel the embrace of Eternity itself!

But rumors of infidelity spread quickly
until one evening, in a jealous rage
Steller buried a hatchet deep between her eyes.
Afterwards he recorded:

When confronted, she refused to confess.
Like her species in toto
she proved mute and reticent, resigned to fate.

Even when mortally wounded,
she could barely manage a bellow.
My beloved died like all her kind before her —
quietly, heaving a deep sigh.

„Vanishing Acts", 2019

Paketboot „Svjatoj Petr" auf Expeditionsfahrt, 1741
Motiv einer Briefmarke der Post der UdSSR, 1966

Auf der „St. Peter" fuhren Kapitan-Komandor Vitus
Bering als Kapitän des Schiffes und Kommodore der
Expeditionsschiffe, Leutnant Sven Waxell als sein I.
Offizier und Wilhelm Steller als Arzt und
Naturforscher.

47

STELLER'S DREAM
by Jennifer Chang

Asleep, I lived
in silence, but in light.
What, if waking were a room
black as the mind? Hornbilled dream
Steller's dream. And the body,
a darkness there is no memory of.

„Slept", 2014

STELLERS TRAUM
von Jennifer Chang, übersetzt von Joachim Ruf

Schlafend lebte ich
in der Stille, aber im Licht.
Was, wenn Wachen ein Raum wäre,
schwarz wie der Verstand? Traum von einem
Hornschnabel.
Stellers Traum. Und der Körper
eine Dunkelheit. Es gibt keine Erinnerung daran.

STELLERS GEBET
von Andrej Bronnikov

О Господи, неисповедимы пути Твои,
и каждый, кто хочет увидеть Тебя,
увидит Тебя. И я, прошедший полмира,
вступаю в Твои владенья, и Твой свет
озаряет меня.

Горизонт, твоя черта подводит итог моей жизни.

Десяток новых растений, несколько рыб, три зверька

(Морская корова 10 м длиной и весит 5 тонн,

если это

имеет значенье).

Шестнадцать ящиков коллекций. Две или три

птицы.

Сотня гербариев (мечта Крашенниникова и

Линнея).

Шесть пар башмаков, истоптанных за жизнь.

Две написанных книги. Один иностранный язык

(Русский), не считая латыни. 25 неотправленных

писем.

Одна любовь. Два учителя. Корабль с умирающими

Солдатами и остров с умирающими моряками.

Один командор, не дошедший до порта.

Тюрьма. Два ареста по ложным доносам.

Враги и друзья. Пять новых гор. Две реки.

Один остров.

Скала, похожая на каменные ворота.

Лютеранская Библия, подарок отца.

Молитва Св. Петру, услышанная Св. Петром.

Спасение. Одиночество. Чего желать больше?

Я сижу и смотрю, как этот Богом забытый трактир

Превращается в свадебный дом в Галилее, и входит

Один, превращавший воду в вино, присаживается

ко мне

И говорит: Георг, ты сделал, наверное, все.

И я знаю, что это – конец. Но в Божьих руках

не чувствую страха.

„Исчезающий Вид“, 2008/2009

STELLERS GEBET
von A. Bronnikov, übersetzt von Christine Hengevoß

*O Herr, unerforschlich sind DEINE Wege, und jeder, der
DICH erblicken will, wird DICH erblicken. Auch ich, der ich
die halbe Welt durchquert habe, trete ein in DEIN Reich, und
DEIN Licht wird mich erleuchten.*

Horizont, deine Linie zieht die Bilanz meines
Lebens.

Zehn neue Pflanzen, mehrere Fische, drei Tiere

(die Seekuh 10 Meter lang, mit einem Gewicht von

5 Tonnen, falls das von Bedeutung ist).

Sechzehn Kästen mit Sammlungen. Zwei oder drei
Vögel.

Hundert Herbarien (ein Traum für

Krascheninnikow und Linné)
Im Leben sechs paar Schuhe ausgetreten.
Zwei Bücher geschrieben. Eine Fremdsprache
(Russisch), Latein nicht mitgerechnet.
25 unabgesandte Briefe.
Eine Liebe. Zwei Lehrer. Ein Schiff mit sterbenden
Soldaten und eine Insel mit sterbenden Seeleuten.
Ein Kommandeur, der es nicht bis zum Hafen
geschafft hat.
Gefängnis. Zwei Verhaftungen aufgrund falscher
Denunziationen.
Feinde und Freunde. Fünf neue Berge.
Zwei Flüsse. Eine Insel.
Ein Felsen, der aussieht wie ein Tor.
Eine Lutherbibel, Geschenk des Vaters.
Ein Gebet an St. Peter, von St. Peter erhört.
Rettung. Einsamkeit. Was will ich mehr?
Ich sitze da und schaue zu, wie diese gottverlassene
Kaschemme
sich in das Hochzeitshaus von Galiläa verwandelt,
und herein kommt
Einer, der Wasser in Wein verwandelt hat,
setzt sich zu mir
und sagt: Georg, du hast wahrscheinlich
alles erledigt.

Auch ich weiß: Dies ist das Ende.
Doch in Gottes Händen
verspüre ich keine Furcht.

**Gräber der Besatzung der „Svjatoj Petr" von 1741
auf der Beringinsel, 2018**

Gedichte über Stellers Seekuh
(Steller's Sea Cow)

Plakat zur Ausrottung der Stellerschen Seekuh
im Wiener Naturhistorischen Museum

STELLER'S SEA COW
by Eleni Sikelianos

By night, the gomuls took to the skies
to hunt & returned with a whale
impaled on each enormous finger
The volcanoes lit up for the roasting
Captain Vitus Bering landed in a storm– then died
As to his shipmates the meat of the sea cow
kept them alive
Georg Steller drew & described:
„Its skin is black and thick,
like the bark of an old oak";
4-5 fathoms long, 3.5 fathoms round,
weight: 200 puds.
It drifted just below the surface of the water
close to shore
„a single animal resembled an overturned boat,"
and they stripped its skin for barks
the last cow was killed for its excellent meat
Had they been mistaken for sirens
would the flesh have been so sweet

„Make Yourself happy", 2017

One fathom is 6 feet; 200 puds is about 8,000 pounds.
Lonely sailors are said to have mistaken manatees for sirens.

REQUIEM FÜR EINE SEEKUH
von Heinrich Detering

Im Jahr 1741 fand Steller die Stellersche Seekuh
(Hydrodamalis gigas)
auf der Bering- und der Kupferinsel sie gehörte
zu den letzten ihrer neuentdeckten Art
ihr riesenhaftes Gerippe zeigte er in Wien
siebzigtausend Jahre lang hatte die Stellersche Seekuh
schweigsam geweidet in Algen und Tang
in Wärmeperioden in Kältephasen im Tauwasser der
Eiszeit
im flachen Wasser vor der Kamtschatka
siebzigtausend Jahre lang das sanfteste Tier
acht Meter lang warmpelzig wehrlos
als der erste Mensch
sie fand im flachen Wasser vor der Kamtschatka dem
Weide-
dem Jagdgrund
das sanfteste Tier die leichteste Beute
sie war schmackhaft und zart
wie Menschenfleisch
nach siebenundzwanzig Jahren
war die letzte getötet und verzehrt
man kann sie betrachten im Naturkundemuseum in
Wien
ohne Pelz ohne Fleisch und noch immer ganz still.

„Old Glory", 2012

STELLER'S SEA COW, 1742 – 1768
by Tom Sexton

Steller took it as a sign from a benevolent God
when he killed the first sea cow. Commander
Bering was dead. The shipwrecked crew had
skin as white as the paper he used to sketch
„that marvelous beast that moved across a bed
of kelp the way a cow moves across a field
before it raised its head and snorted like a horse."
Steller sketched. He would be remembered now.

They boiled its flesh to give them strength.
Scurvy was the ghost that haunted them.
Those who made it back to Siberia told
of a land to the east and a fabulous cow
whose flesh would feed a crew of otter
hunters for a year while they collected pelts
so fine and soft the Czar would envy them.
„Its flesh was tender veal, its fat was almond oil."
Wounded, the last calf sank before it disappeared.

„For the Sake of the Light", 2009

DIE STELLERSCHE SEEKUH, 1742 – 1768
von Tom Sexton, übersetzt von Joachim Ruf

Steller nahm es als Zeichen eines
wohlwollenden Gottes,

als er die erste Seekuh tötete.
Commander Bering war tot.
Die schiffbrüchige Mannschaft hatte eine
Haut, die so weiss war wie das Papier,
auf dem er skizzierte
„dieses wunderbare Tier,
das sich über ein Bett aus Kelp bewegt,
wie eine Kuh über ein Feld zieht,
bevor es+ den Kopf hebt und
wie ein Pferd schnaubt“,
skizzierte Steller.
Er würde jetzt in Erinnerung bleiben.
Sie kochten sein Fleisch, um ihnen
Stärke zu geben.
Skorbut war der Geist, der sie heimsuchte.
Diejenigen, die es zurück nach Sibirien schafften,
erzählten von einem Land im Osten und
einer fabelhaften Kuh, deren Fleisch eine
Mannschaft von Otterjägern
für ein Jahr ernähren würde,
während sie Felle sammelten,
so fein und weich, dass der Zar sie beneiden würde.

„Sein Fleisch war zartes Kalbfleisch,
sein Fett war Mandelöl“.
Verwundet sank das letzte Kalb,
bevor es verschwand.

THE KELP EATERS HYDRODAMALIS GIGAS
by John Glenday

These beasts are four fathoms long, but perfectly
gentle.
They roam the shallower waters like sea-cattle

and graze on the waving flags of kelp.
At the slightest wound their innards will flop

out with a great hissing sound,
but they have not yet grown to fear mankind:

no matter how many of their number might be
killed,
they never try to swim away, they are so mild.

When one is speared, its neighbours will rush in
And struggle to draw out the harpoon

with the blade of their little hooves.
They almost seem to have a grasp of what it is to
love.

I once watched a bull return to its butchered
mate two days in a row, butting its flensed hide

and calling out quietly across the shingle till the
darkness fell.
The flesh on the small calves tastes as sweet as
veal

and their fat is pleasantly coloured,
like the best Dutch butter.

The females are furnished with long, black teats.
When brushed hard with a fingertip

even on the dead
they will grow firm and the sweet milk bleed.

From „Journal of a Voyage with Bering 1741-1742"
By Georg Wilhelm Steller

„Grain", 2009

HYDRODAMALIS GIGAS
von Andrej Bronnikov

Этот остров не видел леса. Как и, впрочем, людей.
Ветер, соль, остающаяся на губах. Песок.
Бухта закрыта с трех сторон. А с четвертой – море.
Что чернеет там между камней? Тюлень?
Отполированный морем валун? Нет, он движется.
Я подхожу, а ему все равно. Гигантских размеров
Зверь. Добродушно пыхтит, крутя головой.
Вот находка. Для этого стоило забросить пение
В хоре прихода в Виндсхайме. Оставить страну,
Отца, мать, учителя, братьев.
Оставить в заснеженном
Северном граде жену. Для этого стоило
Не есть и не спать последние восемь лет.
Это – мой зверь. Ничего, что неловок на вид.
Должно быть, гигантский *Dugongidae*.
Исчезающий вид.
Выглядывает из воды. Косит глазом полуслепым.
Не описан никем. Вот и встретились мы.
Я и зверь, носящий имя мое отныне.
Кожа в морщинах. Удобна для паразитов.
Оттого эти чайки сходят с ума, когда зверь выгибает
Спину. Налетают всей стаей. Хвост раздвоен,
будто
у Ламантина. Но больше. Гораздо больше.
Подхожу еще ближе. Не видит меня, увлечен едою.
Морская капуста. Все камни покрыты ею.
Вот так корова. Пасется мирно. Шевелит под водой
Копытом. И шея – как у быка. Я глажу его по спине.
Огромный, спокойный зверь. Сколько лет
мать-природа
Хранила тебя? Вот и встретились мы. Я, и зверь,
Что присвоит себе мое имя. Под северным желтым

Небом мне идет тридцать третий год. Крики чаек,
Как плач детей. Море дышит холодным ветром.
И качается туша коровы морской в воде.
Этот день уходит в бессмертие. Здесь так хорошо.
Но я должен идти. Слышишь крики? Казак мой —
Петруха. На острове так подружились мы,
Он зовет меня барин Георг, а я его —
Петр Максимович.
Он напуган. Боже правый, какая зверюга!
Сколько ж весу в ней? Пудов двести.
Вон, смотри, там еще одна. И еще. Сколько ж их.
Неизвестно. Вся бухта кишит. Вместо волн —
горбатые
Спины. На радость чайкам и нам. Вот так день!
Мурашки бегут по коже. Открытие: новый зверь.
Неисчислимы созданья Твои, Господь. Пойдем же,
Петр Максимович. Пойдем, позовем людей.
Пополудни
Приходим снова. С нами гарпун и сеть.
Забиваем одну
Корову. Тащим ее на берег. У меня готовы приборы.
Метр линейный и скальпель, чтоб взять специмены.
Десять метров длиной и девять — в обхват. Я пишу в
Блок-ноуте ее размеры. Казаки довольны — не будем
Больше голодны. Здесь нам хватит на месяц
с лихом.
Но косит печально коровы глаз. И внутри у меня
Появляется жалость. Чувство несвойственное
Натуралисту. Ах, корова, прости меня.
У нас ведь одно
С тобой имя. Я пришел сюда издалёка.
Ты жила здесь.
И все, что я должен — я был должен узнать тебя.
Корова, когда мы забивали тебя, твой бык молодой
Крутился вокруг, норовя опрокинуть лодку.

Корова, когда мы тащили на берег тебя, он пытался
Порвать веревку. А когда, устав, мы ушли к костру,
Темной ночью беззвездной, он вдруг вылез
на берег,
Неуклюже загребая песок, и подполз к твоей морде.
И так было три дня. А потом он уплыл,
Исчез в темном море. Я стоял и смотрел,
Как луна светит вслед ему, и мне было грустно.
Поутру казаки разделали тушу. Что за вкус, жир –
Голландское масло! Мясо – почти что говяжье,
но не
Портится быстро. Засолив, можно брать его
в плаванье.
Ну а шкуру пустить на чум или лодку скроить
алеутскую.
Вот так зверь. Мы теперь спасены. Мы прокормимся
Здесь до весны. Нас спасет корова, как тех братьев
спасла
Волчица. Экспедиция удалась. Командора нет
с нами.
И многих людей. Но найден подвид ламантина.

„Исчезающий Вид“, 2008/2009

HYDRODAMALIS GIGAS
von A. Bronnikov, übersetzt von Christine Hengevoß

Diese Insel kennt keinen Wald. Auch
keine Menschen.
Auf unseren Lippen Wind und Salz. Sand.
Land umgibt die Bucht von drei Seiten. Von der
vierten – die See.

Dort, hinter den Felsen, etwas Schwarzes!
Eine Robbe?
Ein vom Meer polierter großer Stein? Nein, es
bewegt sich.
Ich gehe zu ihm, ihm ist es gleich. Ein gigantisches
Tier. Gutmütig schnauft es, dreht den Kopf
hin und her.
Was für ein Fund! Dafür hat es sich gelohnt,
das Singen
im Windsheimer Gemeindechor aufzugeben,
das Land zu verlassen,
Vater, Mutter, Lehrer, Brüder. Die Frau
zurückzulassen
in der verschneiten Stadt im Norden.
Acht Jahre lang nicht zu essen, nicht zu schlafen.
Dies ist mein Tier. Es macht nichts, dass es
plump wirkt.
Es ist wohl eine gigantische Dugongida. Eine
verschwindende Art.
Guckt aus dem Wasser raus. Schielt mit fast
blindem Auge.
Noch nie hat jemand sie beschrieben. Jetzt aber
sind wir uns begegnet.
Ich und das Tier, das seit heute meinen Namen
trägt.
Die Haut ist voller Falten. So etwas mögen
Parasiten.
Darum auch sind die Möwen außer sich, sobald
das Tier den Rücken

krümmt. Der ganze Schwarm ist sogleich da.
Die Schwanzflosse gespalten wie
beim Dugong. Doch es ist größer. Sehr viel größer.
Noch näher gehe ich heran. Es sieht mich nicht, ist
mit Fressen beschäftigt.
Seetang. Die Steine sind alle davon bedeckt.
Was für eine Kuh! Sie weidet friedlich.
Unter Wasser
bewegt sie den Huf. Hat einen Hals wie ein Stier.
Ich streichle ihren Rücken.
Ein riesiges, ruhiges Tier. Wie viele Jahre hat
Mutter Natur
dich bewahrt? So sind wir uns begegnet.
Ich und das Tier,
das meinen Namen annimmt. Ich bin
dreiunddreißig,
hier, unter dem gelben Nordhimmel.
Möwengeschrei,
Kinderweinen gleichend. Das Meer atmet kalten
Wind.
Eine tote Seekuh schaukelt im Wasser.
Dieser Tag wird in die Geschichte eingehen.
Schön ist es hier.
Doch ich muss gehen. Hörst du die Rufe?
Das ist Petrucha,
mein Kosak. Wir haben uns angefreundet auf
der Insel.
Er nennt mich Herr Georg, ich ihn
Peter Maximowitsch.

Ganz erschrocken ist er: Großer Gott, so ein
gewaltiges Tier!
Wie viel es wohl wiegt? Zweihundert Pud gewiss.
Sieh nur, da ist noch eine. Und da auch. Wie viele
mögen es sein?
Wer weiß. Die ganze Bucht wimmelt von ihnen.
Anstelle der Wellen
die Buckel der Rücken. Zu unserer und der Möwen
Freude. Was für ein Tag!
Gänsehaut: Eine Entdeckung, ein neues Tier!
Ohne Zahl sind Deine Schöpfungen, o Herr.
Komm,
Peter Maximowitsch. Komm, holen wir die Leute.
Mittags
kehren wir zurück, mit Netz und Harpune.
Wir schießen eine Kuh.
Schleppen sie an Land. Ich habe meine
Geräte dabei.
Ein Metermaß und ein Skalpell, für die Proben.
Zehn Meter Länge, neun Meter Umfang.
Ich schreibe
die Maße in mein Heft. Die Kosaken sind
zufrieden:
Wir brauchen nicht mehr zu hungern. Dies reicht
für einen guten Monat.
Nur das Auge der Kuh schielt mich traurig an.
In mir
regt sich Mitleid. Untypisch für einen
Naturforscher. Verzeih mir, Kuh! Schließlich

tragen wir
denselben Namen. Ich kam von weit her. Du aber
lebtest hier.
Und alles, was ich hätte tun sollen, war, dich
kennenzulernen.
Kuh, als wir dich töteten, umkreiste uns
dein junger Bulle und versuchte das Jollboot
umzustoßen.
Kuh, als wir dich an Land schleppten, versuchte er
das Tau zu zerreißen. Als wir uns erschöpft ans
Feuer setzten
in der dunklen sternenlosen Nacht, kam er
plötzlich an Land und kroch,
ungeschickt durch den Sand paddelnd, zu deiner
Schnauze.
Drei Tage lang. Dann schwamm er fort,
verschwand im dunklen Meer. Ich stand und
sah zu,
wie der Mond ihm nachschien, und ich verspürte
Trauer.
Heute früh haben die Kosaken das Tier zerlegt.
Was für ein Geschmack, das Fett –
die reinste holländische Butter! Das Fleisch ist fast
wie Rindfleisch,
verdirbt aber nicht schnell. Eingesalzen kann man
es auf große Fahrt mitnehmen.
Mit dem Pelz lässt sich eine Jurte bauen oder
ein Boot.

Was für ein Tier! Jetzt sind wir gerettet. Haben
zu essen,
bis zum Frühjahr. Die Kuh rettet uns, so wie
die Wölfin
jene Brüder rettete. Die Expedition ist erfolgreich.
Der Kommandeur ist nicht mehr bei uns.
Auch viele andere. Doch wir haben eine Unterart
der Seekuh entdeckt.

Skelett einer Stellerschen Seekuh
im Naturhistorischen Museum in Wien

STELLER'S SEA COW
by J. Patrick Lewis

Hydrodamalis gigas. Extinct c. 1767. Bering Sea

Big as a mastodon, a cow
Fed for a month three dozen men.
Three dozen men it took to hook
And haul the beast to land, and when

They'd hack with knives and bayonets
Great strips of blubber, there she'd lie
Unmoving on the ice, and let
out something like a human sigh.

Discovered, 1741,
She dwarfed all creatures of the sea,
Except the whale, so let us toast
Sea cows in their enormity.

„Swan Song", 2003

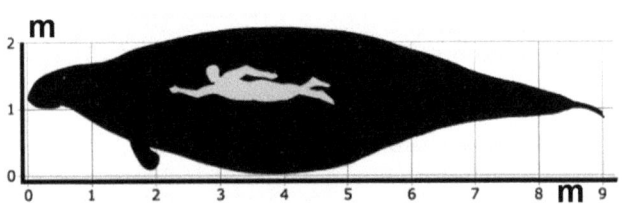

**Größenvergleich zwischen einem Menschen von 1,8 m
Größe und einer Stellerschen Seekuh**
(Nach Anders Jahan Retzius 1794; Prehistoric Wildlife)

DIE STELLER'SCHE SEEKUH

von J. Patrick Lewis, übersetzt von Joachim Ruf

Hydrodamalis gigas. Ausgerottet um 1767. Bering-See

Groß wie ein Mastodon, eine Kuh
Nahrung für einen Monat für drei Dutzend
Männer.
Drei Dutzend Männer, die es brauchte, um sie
einzufangen
Und das Tier an Land zu bringen und wenn

Sie abhackten mit Messern und Bajonetten
große Streifen Speck, da lag sie
Unbeweglich auf dem Eis und ließ
etwas wie einen menschlichen Seufzer
hören.

Entdeckt, 1741,
Sie stellte alle Kreaturen des Meeres
in den Schatten,
Außer dem Wal, lasst uns anstoßen auf
die Seekühe in ihrer Ungeheuerlichkeit.

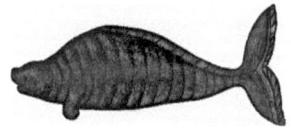

STELLER'S SEA COW
by Anne Marie Macari

Even as they killed them
to extinction, the sea cows
drifted and swam in arctic waters
unafraid of the stranded men.

In the sea cows' parables it was foretold
that extinction comes
into the mind before the body,
a kingdom of oblivion

to swim toward, like the last
passenger pigeon perched
in a zoo, forgetting how
to fly, or a sea cow

slaughtered and dragged to shore, the last
of its kind in the frozen strait –
toothless, spearless,
as the day it was made

but too big to hide. Now they are
parables of themselves
floating in the bloodstreams of humans
who don't even know

they are haunted, followed by sea cows
who watch them as clouds
watch the ocean where the creatures
lived, or by passenger pigeons

who fly into memory, zigzagging
overhead like invisible
schools of fish. …

„Wilderness", 2008

Vulkane auf Kamtschatka
Titelbild zu Stellers
"Beschreibung von dem Lande Kamtschatka"

STELLER'S SEA COW
by Donald Davie

The way to live is on the move.

To wrest from Russia the distinction
Of slaughtering into extinction
Such animals as Steller's sea-
Cow and the sea-otter, he
(So the accepted version goes)
Had the prescience to propose
America dispute the ground
The Russians had, from Nootka Sound,
And thus imperiously invade
The fortune-making peltry trade
That desolated Arctic seas
To warm the backs of Cantonese.
And there's his greatness! What a man
It took, to frame so gross a plan!
What a Napoleon of crime,
Born not before, but of, his time!
Thus the historians, lost in awe
As soon as Nature's rule of law
Is breached on a sufficient scale.
Cachalot and walrus quail.
Prayed after from Connecticut,
Dissolute grave whalers gut
Leviathan's cows, and under Cape

Brett in the Bay of Islands rape
Maori women on the sands
Mauled by Marion's dying hands.

Luckily, none of this is true:
Any nation's flag would do
To plant upon the unexplored,
Unbestowable seaboard
That beckoned Ledyard like a dream,
Unprofitable and extreme.
America and Freedom earn,
It's true, apostrophes à la Sterne
Still, in the desultory pages
That trace him by Siberian stages
Eastward; but after John Paul Jones
And Jefferson fail to raise the loans
He'd hoped to touch them for, occurs
No mention of the trade in furs.

„Six epistles to Eva Hesse", 2002

STELLER'S SEA COW
by Jennifer Dunbar Dorn

Steller and the rest of the men survived
on a diet of anti-scorbutic plants and roots,
sea otter (they brought back at least
700 pelts to sell in Kamchatka),
as well as seals and sea lions,
but these creatures, at first so trusting,
moved further and further away
making the hunters trek for days to find them.

When spring came, they set about
dismantling the ship to build a smaller vessel.
Steller organized crews of men to hunt, cook, carry.
The yawl was also repaired in a determined effort
to haul in meat they saw every day
in the form of huge sea cows.
These 8000 pound, 30 foot long
kelp-eating manatee had hides too thick
and tough to penetrate,
but with a boat, a harpooner,
and 40 men on shore pulling the rope,
they managed to bring one in like a beached whale.

They would kill 12 more before leaving.
The meat was delicious and lasted a long time —
one creature could feed 30 men for a month at sea

without spoiling — the fat was tastier
than butter or olive oil
and the milk better than cream from a cow.
Sadly for the creature who would come
to be known as Steller's sea cow
it took only 27 years for the promyshlenniki,
the trappers and traders who followed in the wake
of the Great Northern Expedition,
to hunt the species out of existence.
Wintering on Bering Island, they'd kill enough
sea cow meat to last them 3 years in America.
The fur rush and commercial greed of
the Russian-American Company
would also decimate the otters and seals
and colonize the people.

„Eastward Ho!", 2015

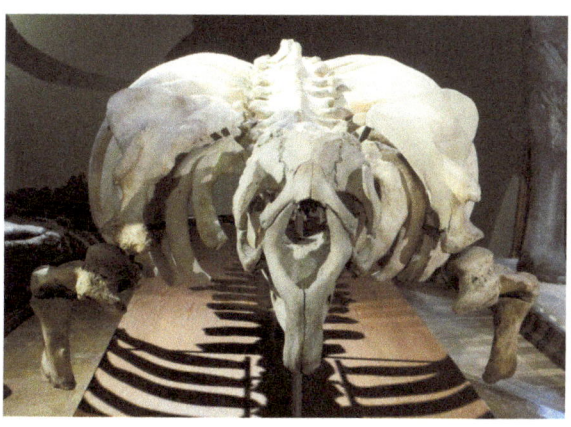

Skelett einer Stellerschen Seekuh
im Naturhistorischen Museum in Wien

DIE STELLER'SCHE SEEKUH
von Mikael Vogel

Auf Stümpfen zog sie sich über den
Boden, weidete Seetang ab, behäbige Kolossin
Neun Meter lang, zehn Tonnen schwer,
Borkenhaut, 18 Kilo Herz.
Zahn- und als einziges Säugetier fingerknochenlos
konnte sie sich nicht wehren
Als Vitus Berings Schiff, von Zar Peter dem
Großen auf Entdeckungsreise befohlen
Eine Landbrücke zwischen Asien und Amerika zu
suchen
Auf ihrer abgelegenen Insel Schiffbruch erlitt,
die Mannschaft hungrig
Über sie herzufallen begann. Bering starb an
Skorbut, der ihn begleitende Naturforscher
Georg Wilhelm Steller aber verkündete nach seiner
Rückkehr auf dem russischen Festland
Ihre Existenz. Das Buffet war eröffnet —
27 Jahre nach ihrer Entdeckung
Erschlugen Robbenjäger die Letzte ihrer Art.
Wegproviant und Öl.
Einige, beschrieb Steller, *schnitten dem noch lebenden
Thiere
Grosse Stücken aus. Die weibliche Scham stehet acht Zoll
über dem Hintern.
In die Spalte selbst gehen fünf zusammen geschlagene Finger
Ohne Zwang*

„Dodos auf der Flucht", 2018

DIE SEEKUH
von Detlev Wilhelm Klee

Gleiten, schlafen, träumen, gleiten,
wenn über die kaum geöffneten Augen
auf flachem, trübem Meergrund Seegras streift
Tang die Arme schwingt um den saugenden Mund …

Oder sie im Wurzellabyrinth der Mangroven
nach Blättern tastet mit den verständigen Haaren,
nach der Wasserhyazinthe blaßlila Blüten …

Gleiten, schlafen, träumen, gleiten …

Die gespaltene oder halbmondförmige Fluke
rudert die bedächtige Kuh ins Helle,
um Atem zu schöpfen über dem Schaum –
hört sie, wie die schmale Lippe des Horizonts tönt,
oder der Winde mythengrünes Rauschen?

Gleiten, schlafen, träumen, gleiten …

Sie wirbelt Schleier feinen Sands um sich auf,
als wäre die Muschelstille, die Andacht
still kauenden Lebens nicht tief genug …

Der Schatten des Jungtiers umspielt sie
mit sanfter Kühle, wickelt sie ein
in die Langmut des ruhelosen Nomaden …

Oder die Lebensfreude, die Nähe
von Mutter und Kind, ertönt in Duetten
hohen Zwitscherns und Pfeifens …

Sind die Rhythmen der herrischen Sonne,
der Gezeiten Wogen und Ebben,
sind ihr die Landschaft der fetten Weiden
von Seegras und blauen Algen

oder die Schattenmale der Menschen
auf den Wanderdünen der Zeit
zu Bildern erwacht im Traum?

Gleiten, schlafen, träumen, gleiten …

Sind das hohe Glimmen des Sternlichts,
das bleiche Tränengesicht des Monds
und das grüne Irrlicht der Nacht,
sind ihr die Nixen, Sirenen, Melusinen,
ihre Schwestern am Bugspriet der Schiffe
von Hanno dem Karthager bis Erik dem Roten,
von Christoph Kolumbus bis Vasco da Gama
zu Bildern erwacht im Schlaf?

Gleiten, schlafen, träumen, gleiten …

Weiche Nymphe des Meers,
bist du Askalons Fischweib,
die graue Göttin der Vorwelt,
der Semiramis Mutter,
homerische Nereide,
die ihre traurigen Zitzen reckt
aus dem versunkenen Reich der Sage?

Die müden Lider decken den Tag ihr zu,
den dämmrigen, sie kennt nicht der Herkunft
Grotten, erhellt vom Gesang der Flammen,
nicht Nester der Heimat, schwebend
von weichen Daunen der Liebe.

Für immer Verstandesnetzen unfaßbar,
erlischt sie, ein Irrwisch,
flieht sie, ein Schatten, dahin.

Gleiten, schlafen, träumen, gleiten …

„Lux autumnalis", 2016

EXTINCTION NARRATIVE
by Jason Zuzga

So this is what it feels like
to be crowded into the body
of a Steller's Sea Cow.

It's moving along the tidal rocks
munching on sea lettuce the color
of absinthe. Chartreuse.

You are shifting next to me
trying to get comfortable.
Even though this extinct body is eight meters long,
it's a tight fit for two young homosexuals.

The skin is so thick that the icy waters
of the Bering Sea don't register at all.

I feel the warm flesh on my face.
I can feel your arm around
me. I can feel thumps echo from
other Sea Cows, nuzzling ours.

Here come those intrepid explorers.
Let us be pointless.

„Heat Wake", 2016

STELLER'S SEA COWS
by Timothy Donnelly

*...There were no Steller's sea cows, the tame
kelp-nibbling cousins to the manatee, albeit double their size,*

*and there were no great auks. The last known pair of them
was claimed on July 3, 1844 by poachers hired by a merchant
itching for tchotchkes to ornament an office. Three long
winters later, rescue sledges bundled McClure and crew up
and sped them back to the claps of Britain. Soon Banks Island's
musk ox population whittled down to nil as their flesh gave*

*way to the hungry Inuit who trekked up to 300 miles to strip
McClure's abandoned ship before the ice crushed her completely,
folding her metals into Mercy Bay. "I took him by the neck
and he flapped his wings," the poacher said. "He made no cry."
Inuit shaped Investigator's copper and iron into spear- and arrow-
heads as well as knife blades, chisels, and harpoons like those*

depicted in lithographs in the mitts of seal hunters patiently

*stationed at breathing holes in the ice. But there were no
broad-leaved centaury plants, no western sassafras, and no
Galapagos amaranth, cousin to the seabeach amaranth. Its tiny
spinach-like leaves once bounced along dunes from South
Carolina to Massachusetts till habitat loss, insensitive beach-*

grooming tactics, and recreational vehicles slashed figures
drastically. When ice decides it must feel like being splintered
from a multiplex of tightness that pains but holds together.
Aerial shot of 1961. Year submarine thriller K-19 and Saving
Mr. Banks are set in. Kennedy is president. The cloud of a
hundred
musk oxen migrating back to Banks Island rises plainly as

narrow-leafed campion, a handful of whose seeds had slept
30 millennia before being found in 2007 in a ruined system of
ground squirrel burrows. Surveys will report up to 800
heads in 1967 and a thousand more in 1970. All matter
thunder-
cracking belowdecks: hoof of earth into water, water over
air, air under water and up. So that the vessel, broken, settles

onto sea stars on the floor. The seeds were sown successfully
under grow lights in Siberia, deep in whose permafrost
international high-fiving scientists discovered a fully intact
woolly mammoth carcass. To enlarge my sympathy I attempt
to picture the loud tarp tents around the digging site, the lamp-
lengths they putter away to, the costs.

Auszug aus
„The Hymn to Life", 2014

SIREN SONG
by David Day

Steller's Sea Cow – Extinct 1768 – Hydrodamalis gigas –
Bering Sea

Some still nights
On the shores of Bering's sea
You may imagine them

Huge as the hull
Of an overturned ship
Moaning in the rolling surf

Fountain of hot blood pulsing
Furnace of the deep heart
Wave-worn giants, idle lovers
On the swell of the sea

Bigger than elephants
Skin like the bark of an ancient oak
Snorting like horses
Pawing the kelp meadows
With their tough hooves
Like bulls in pasture

Tide riders, storm biders
Slow to lust as elephants
Passionate as whales

Beauty here in a thing not itself beautiful
As delight in the play of light
On a mountain or a great rock
Yet something vastly alive
As these once were alive

Some still nights
On the shores of Bering's sea
You may imagine them

The great breath-song
Through the sighing night

„Nevermore", 2012

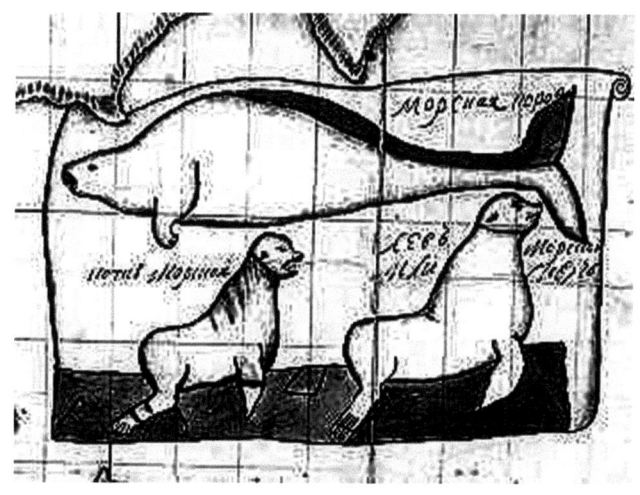

„Pekarskische Abbildung"
Älteste Darstellung von Stellers Seekuh nach seinem Bericht
auf der Seekarte von Sofron Khitrov und Sven Waxell
1743/44, veröffentlicht 1893.

mild
by Tom Clark

They're easy together
inside the pod
when there's no hunting
the yelp of the little
one is not heard
on good days

when the weather is mild they move
like the vowels in the word
repose
off shore to browse
among sea
urchin and mussel
encrusted submerged reefs
or in drifting patches of
floating kelp

"Empire of Skin", 1997

Der Seeotter wurde erstmals 1741 auf der Großen
Nordischen Expedition entdeckt und von Steller in dem
Kapitel "De bestiis marinis" in "Novi Commentarii" der
Akademie der Wissenschaften in St. Petersburg von
1751 und seiner "Beschreibung von sonderbaren
Meerthieren", 1753 ausführlich beschrieben und zudem
illustriert.

**Stellers „Sonderbare Meerthiere", 1753 und
ein „Meerotter" an Land und im Wasser, 1751**

SEA OTTER HUNT
by Mary Lilly Kienholz

Behold the far ship,
where the blue waves are curling,
Its anchor on deck,
Its mainsailunfurling,
And, round it, bidarkas
Not far from the shore,
All manned by Aleuts.
There's a thousand or more.

The ship, like a swan
With its cygnets around,
Is prepared to sail off
Where the boatmen can circle
For one-sided battles,
With Aleut „throwing board"
And harpoons called atlatls.

The wages rewarded.
For deftness, and leads
To the seaotters' „rafts",
Will be cartons of beads:
Beads sky-blue and green,
Beads purple and red –
Beads red as the blood
That the sea otters shed.

„Adventures in Poetry", 2010

KOMÖDIE VOM MEEROTTER
von Mikael Vogel

In Kelpwald
Snack in der Hand
Auf dem Rücken durchs Leben treibend im
dichtesten Fell aller
Tiere… von Wogen sanft gehoben gesenkt bis
Die Entdeckung durch Steller auch ihn mit ihrem
Fluch be-
Legte. Landratten eilten auf
Mit Lederriemen zu Booten verschnürten Planken
an um ihn
Totzuprügeln, den wertvollsten Pelz zu tausenden
wegzuschleppen.
Die russischen Populationen in 60 Jahren
annihiliert
Vor Kalifornien ent-
Brannte der Pelzgoldrausch neu bis die Jagd auf die
wenigen Letzten 1911
Nicht mehr lohnte, Pelzhändler gegen ein Schutz-
gesetz keinen Widerstand aufboten
Der letzte legal gehandelte Pelz in London eine
Rekordsumme einbrachte.
Wo der Meerotter verschwunden war explodierte
die Zahl von Seeigeln

Aßen ungestört die Seetangwälder vom
Meeresgrund bis hoch in die Wellen weg, Unter-
wasserwüste zurücklassend.
Tauchte vor Alaska wieder auf wo
Am 24. März 1989 die Exxon Valdez havarierte, er
im ausströmenden Öl
Mit Seelöwen, Robben, Fischen, Schildkröten,
Seevögeln, Delphinen, Walen
Erstickte, vergiftet verendete. Erfror.
Heute von Orcas
Dezimiert — sie können keine
Größere Nahrung mehr
Finden

„Dodos auf der Flucht", 2018

Steller vermisst eine Seekuh.
Zeichnung von Stejneger, 1925

STELLER'S SEA COW SPEAKS
by Fama

Nature made me
But I feel as if I've lost protection

Nature made me
Yet I feel as if nature itself
doesn't know who I am

Nature made me
But I'm under constant threat
from those superior to me

Nature made me
Somehow I had this natural feeling
that you too would care enough for me

Nature made me
So I thought you would love me
as your fellow companion

Nature made me
And for my fate there was zero creation
because now it ends.

„Extinction Poems", 2011

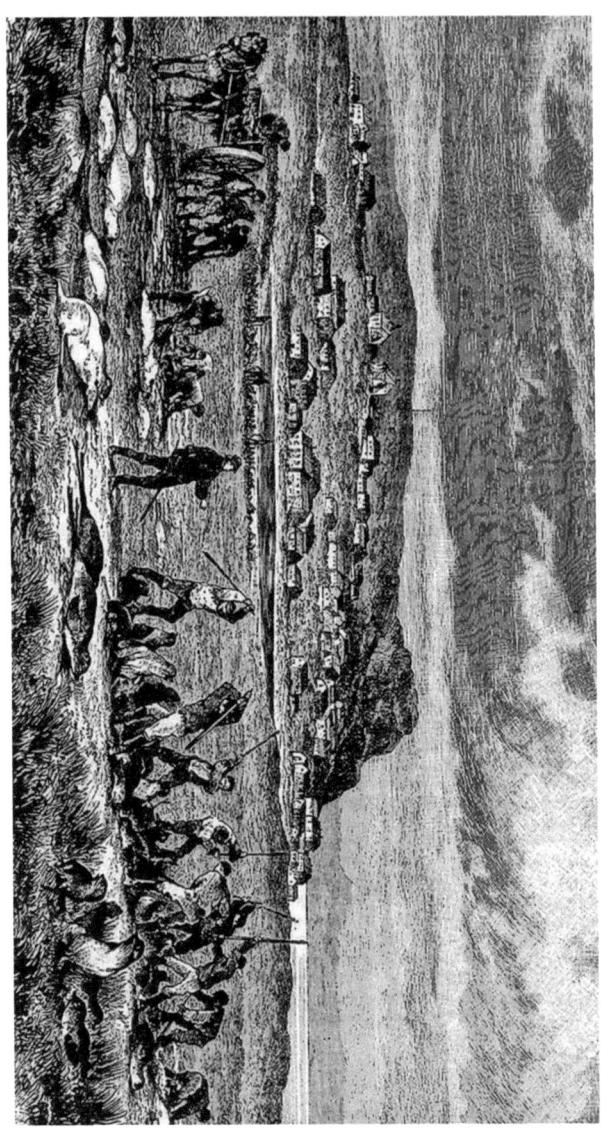

Pelztierjagd auf der Insel St. Paul

Gedichte über den Stellerschen Häher (Steller's Jay)

Der Stellersche Schwarzkopf- oder Diademhäher (Cyanocitta stelleri) ist vom südlichen Alaska aus im westlichen Bereich von Nord- und Mittelamerika bis nach El Salvador anzutreffen. Seine Unterarten unterscheiden sich nach Größe und Färbung.

Unterarten

Cyanocitta stelleri annectens
Cyanocitta stelleri carbonacea
Cyanocitta stelleri carlottae
Cyanocitta stelleri frontalis
Cyanocitta stelleri macrolopha
Cyanocitta stelleri stelleri

STELLER'S JAY
by Robert Hass

The haiku comes
in threes
with the virtues of brevity:
What a strange thing!
To be alive
beneath plum blossoms.
The black-headed
Steller's jay is squawking
in our plum.
Thief! Thief!
A hard, indifferent bird.
he'd snatch your life.

„Songs to Survive the Summer", 1979

Stellerscher Schwarzkopfhäher

STELLER'S JAY
by Tom Sexton

A strong wind has stripped
the crab apple of its sour fruit.

I watch a Steller's jay take one
peck, complain, and adjust

its lustrous blue-black cape.
When it spots me watching

from the window, it tilts
its head in my direction

as if it were a naturalist about
to give me an ill-fitting name.

„For the Sake of the Light", 2009

STELLER'S JAY
by Linda Bierds

Georg Steller, The American Expedition, 1742

From the Harbor of Apostles Peter and Paul,
we sailed in their namesakes, St. Peter
with its groats and falconets, St. Paul
with its groats and falconets,
then ship and ship in a topgallant wind
bearing east-southeast togeteher, identical to the
distant eye
as glimmer and reflection.

*　　　　　*

When we shall wish to speak to you, Captain —
and Captain —
to warn you or guide you or follow or precede you,
we shall, through pennants, jacks, drums, bells,
lanterns, guns and speaking horns,
deliver a language precise as script,
through which may God preserve us.

*　　　　　*

Light rain. Open sea.
I think of the rhumb we have set for ourselves
as ice upon a pin tip: point and course
interchangeable. Now and then,

from the pitch pot, the faintest scent of pine.
St. Paul in the east all morning.

*   *

If we should desire that you take the lead …
If you should desire to lower the yards …
If it is desired to anchor in fog …
If we should separate –
from which misfortune may God preserve us …

If after three days …
If from the flagstaff a blue flag …
If in sailing close-hauled or free …

*   *

What good is structure against a world
already structured by chaos? What good,
pattern, sequence, formation, formality?
We lost the St. Paul on the sixteenth day,
though we sensed thereafter a parallel presence.

Four months. Clewed. Hove to.
Then islands and islands at the New World's rim.
What else can I tell you?

Shipwreck. Rocks on the boot soles. Down the
beach,

one arctic fox, fearless, barked.

*   *

Presence? Parallel. A thereafter sensed. We, though

. . .

Then more, barking, white in their winter fur,
slinking in toward our fires like ground fog.
They had no history with us, and hence
no fear of us, we with so little but history.

We shot them. They came. We shot. They came.
When winter blew through our crude huts,
we caulked the sticks with their bodies.
When blizzards drove us deep in their caves.

They climbed into crevices over our heads, shifting
all night like a wind-rippled canopy –
or wide-winged, otherworldly bird
that would not fly from us.

*   *

When we shall lay to … you shall lay to …
When we after drifting … you after drifting …
When we shall lower … you shall lower …

*   *

To lay, drifting lower. After drifting to rise …
As, God willing, they do, sounding their way
down these shallow coasts, echo by echo.

Scurvy and winter lessened us, already
halved on the sixteenth day –

not from ourselves, exactly, or from others,
but from the outcome of self and other,
the crafted, patterned offerings
that, over water, met us halfway.

What else can I tell you, there in your morning
or nightfall, knowing already
of voyages, violence, hardship, grace? What else
can I write, alive and whole and world-full,
yet fractured as these notes to you?

From the body of our ship, collapsed on the shore,
we built a ship, from the shattered shape
a smaller shape, a single-masted oval cask
which, over time, delivered us.

*   *

Two lanterns, that we might receive you …
Six guns, that we might avoid you …
One flag – blue – that we might know you
after long absence …

*   *

They seem nothing but steam now, the foxes.
The sudden, unbidden breath over glass
that blinds us shapelessly.

What most endures with me –
a multi-voiced jay – will, you say,

carry what most remains of me. My name
and the bird stitched back to back, balanced

as reflection. S – t – e – l – l – e – r' – s   j – a – y
– four strokes plus a star mark reaching upward,
five strokes in answer close to the ground,
one stroke, then one
fathoming, and the whole, aloft on the thermals,
blue as the pennants that reveal from the crosstrees
we are each the lost companion.

„The Journal", 2013
„Roget's Illusion", 2014

STELLER'S JAY
by Wallace Kaufman

Almost 300 years ago
Wilhelm Georg Steller saw
A bird as blue as indigo.
As I write of Steller's life
that bird in sun or snow
brightens every day
with color and his memory.
His grave at Tyumen washed away
His bones again went out to sea
I feed his bird each day.
And Steller's jay feeds me.

(Note: Those who know Steller's life and death will know that his body apparently washed out of the banks of the Tura River and presumably out to sea)

Erste Publikation.
Vgl. „Sic Vita", 2019

EVENING : STELLER'S JAY
by Jory Mickelson

Often, day goes sweetly as a bird
returning to the branch it loves
most to watch the waters

of the lake on lazy afternoons.
Say the tree is a shade
oak. Say the bird's not

a bird at all, but a boy
who's learned to keep
his wings. He spends his few

hours crossing water from one bend
of shore to the other, sometimes
just to hear the gravel

grate against the hull
as he pulls the boat to shore.
Say the boy isn't pulling

a boat at all, but swimming
with one arm holding the late
afternoon's gold aloft, an offering

like time crossed out slowly
one square to the next, an Xing,
the flared tail of the Steller's

jay who returns to
her young no matter
what has sent her flashing away.

„Plenitude", 2018

ODE TO A STELLER'S JAY
by Jeremy Schwartz

Hop, hop, hop, you move effortlessly from branch
to branch.

Wings flutter, but seem barely needed as you
descend. Limb by limb, eyes always on your next
move.

A hood and cloak of black, a highwayman's jacket
for a highwayman's bird, covering bold blue be-
neath. A crest, streaked with sky blue reaching to-
ward the heavens.

Hard not to notice you.

Eyes piercing, as you glare from your perch.
Warning call like a siren, announcing your presence.
Gaze locked on us, telling us to beware. Mammals
and birds alike keep their distance, you say.

Your yard, your turf. You've made this your space.

„Medium's Daily Digest", 2017

STELLER'S JAY
NOT YOUR ORDINARY BLUE BIRD

by Joanne Stolen

If you catch a glimpse of a large,
iridescent, blue bird flitting
around in the trees,
it is probably a Steller's Jay.
This striking bird has a long,
prominent, shaggy crest on its head and a long tail.
The front of its body is black, and the black
extends midway down its back
with the wings a sparkling or iridescent blue.
This jay is named after the German naturalist
Georg Wilhelm Steller.
I had always thought
it was called "stellar" jay with an "a" for its
brilliant coloration.

„Summit Outside", 2011

AUTUMN PSALM
by Jacqueline Osherow

A full year passed (the seasons keep me honest)
since I last noticed this same commotion.
Who knew God was an abstract expressionist?

I'm asking myself — the very question
I asked last year, staring out at this array
of racing colors, then set in motion

by the chance invasion of a Steller's jay.
Is *this* what people mean by *speed of light?*
My usually levelheaded mulberry tree

hurling arrows everywhere in sight —
its bow: the out-of-control Virginia creeper
my friends say I should do something about,

whose vermilion went at least a full shade deeper
at the provocation of the upstart blue,
the leaves (half green, half gold) suddenly hyper

in savage competition with that red and blue —
tohubohu returned, in living color.
Kandinsky: where were you when I needed you?

My attempted poem would lie fallow a year;
I was so busy focusing on the desert's
stinginess with everything but rumor.

No place even for the spectrum's introverts —
rose, olive, gray — no pigment at all —
and certainly no room for shameless braggarts

like the ones that barge in here every fall
and make me feel like an unredeemed failure
even more emphatically than usual.

And here they are again, their fleet allure
still more urgent this time — the desert's gone;
I'm through with it, want something fuller —

why shouldn't a person have a little fun,
some utterly unnecessary extravagance?
Which was — at least I think it was — God's plan

when He set up (such things are never left
to chance)
that one split-second assignation
with genuine, no-kidding-around omnipotence

what, for lack of better words, I'm calling *vision*.
You breathe in, and, for once, there's something
there.
Just when you thought you'd learned some
resignation,

there's real resistance in the nearby air
until the entire universe is swayed.
Even that desert of yours isn't quite so bare

and God's not nonexistent; He's just been waylaid
by a host of what no one could've foreseen.
He's got plans for you: this red-gold-green parade

is actually a fairly detailed outline.
David never needed one, but he's long dead
and God could use a little recognition.

He promises. It won't go to His head
and if you praise Him properly (an autumn psalm!
Why didn't *I* think of that?) you'll have it made.

But while it's true that my Virginia creeper praises
Him,
its palms and fingers crimson with applause,
that the local breeze is weaving Him a diadem,

inspecting my tree's uncut gold for flaws,
I came to talk about the way that violet-blue
sprang the greens and reds and yellows

into action: actual motion. I swear it's true
though I'm not sure I ever took it in.
Now I'd be prepared, if some magician flew

into my field of vision, to realign
that dazzle out my window yet again.
It's not likely, but I'm keeping my eyes open

though I still wouldn't be able to explain
precisely what happened to these vines, these trees.
It isn't available in my tradition.

For this, I would have to be Chinese,
Wang Wei, to be precise, on a mountain,
autumn rain converging on the trees,

a cassia flower nearby, a cloud, a pine,
washerwomen heading home for the day,
my senses and the mountain so entirely in tune

that when my stroke of blue arrives, I'm ready
Though there is no rain here: the air's shot through
with gold on golden leaves. Wang Wei's so giddy

he's calling back the dead: *Li Bai! Du Fu!*
Guys! You've got to see this – autumn sun!
They're suddenly hell-bent on learning Hebrew

in order to get inside the celebration,
which explains how they wound up where they are
in my university library's squashed domain.

Poor guys, it was Hebrew they were looking for,
but they ended up across the aisle from Yiddish —
some Library of Congress cataloger's sense of
humor:

the world's calmest characters and its most skittish
squinting at each other, head to head,
all silently intoning some version of kaddish

for their nonexistent readers, one side's dead
(the twentieth century's lasting contribution
and the other's insufficiently learned

to understand a fraction of what they mean.
The writings in the world's most spoken language
across from one that can barely get a minyan.

Sick of *lanzmen,* the *yidden* are trying to engage
the guys across the aisle in some conversation:
How, for example, do you squeeze an image

into so few words, respectfully asks Glatstein.
Wang Wei, at first, doesn't understand the
problem
but then he shrugs his shoulders, mumbles *Zen*

… but, please, I, myself, overheard a poem,
in the autumn rain, once, on a mountain.
How do you do it? I believe it's called a psalm?

Glatstein's cronies all crack up in unison.
Okay, groise macher, give him an answer.
But Glatstein dons his yarmulke (who knew he
had one?)

and starts the introduction to the morning prayer,
Pisukei di zimrah, psalm by psalm.
Wang Wei is spellbound, the stacks' stale air

suddenly a veritable balm
and I'm so touched by these amazing goings-on
that I've forgotten all about the autumn

staring straight at me: still alive, still golden.
What's gold, anyway, compared to poetry?
a trick of chlorophyll, a trick of sun.

True. It was something, my changing tree
with its perfect complement: a crimson vine,
both thrown into panic by a Steller's jay,

but it's hard to shake the habit of digression.
Wandering has always been my people's way
whether we're in a desert or narration.

It's too late to emulate Wang Wei
and his solitary years on that one mountain
though I'd love to say what I set out to say

just once. Next autumn, maybe. *What's the occasion?*
Glatstein will shout over to me from the bookcase
(that is, if he's paying any attention)

and, finally, I'll look him in the face.
Quick. Out the window, Yankev. It's here again.

„The Hoopoe's Crown", 2005

AMERICAN BLUE JAY – JULY 20, 1741

by Jennifer Dunbar Dorn

Hardly had I climbed ashore
and walked along the coast a bit
before I saw the remains of a fire
with bones, meat, dried fish and mussels
lying about. There were also shells
with sweet grass over which water
had been poured to extract the sweetness —
just as the Kamchadals did. Possibly
these natives emigrated from there.
Further on I came across a place
strewn with cut grass and underneath
a covering of rocks over timber.
Below I found a dug-out cellar 2 fathoms deep
with the following items in it:
receptacles made of stripped bark filled with
smoked salmon;
sweet grass; other grass skinned like hemp,
for fishnets perhaps;
bundles of straps made from seaweed;
arrows scraped very smooth and painted black.
I sent back samples with my Cossack
with instructions to ask the Captain-Commander
for assistance in further exploring the region.

I then covered the cellar
and continued my investigations.
Further on, from the top of a hill,
I saw smoke rising from a breezy knoll
covered with conifers.
Hurrying back to shore I sent word
with the boat just then returning
to ask the Captain-Commander for a small yawl
and several men for a few hours.
Meanwhile, on the beach, by the stream,
utterly exhausted, I described the rarest plants
which I was afraid would wilt,
and revived myself by checking out
the excellent water for tea.
An hour later I got his gracious answer:
I was to get my ass on board immediately.

While I continued to collect plant specimens
and gather anti-scorbutic flora
as an antidote to the scurvy
which is draining the strength
of the men from day to day,
I sent Thomas to shoot some rare birds,
and as luck would have it he brought
back one that looks like an American blue jay.
I recognized it from a painting by Catesby
in a book published recently in London,

a copy of which I'd seen at the Academy.
Unlike the European and Siberian
species, the plumage is brilliantly
blue — without the rusty tail feathers
of the latter and with a tufted crown
not worn by the former species.
At sunset, after further excursions
into forests of giant spruce trees and hemlocks,
I was ordered to return or else . . .
Knowing the Captain-Commander's
antipathy to my botanizing,
and the lack of space on the ship,
of the 135 plants I observed and described,
I brought back only 3 specimens,
one a bush of exceptionally large
and exquisite tasting berries.
I was not surprised, when we got back,
to be greeted with a great guffaw as
the Captain set the plants aside.
But then, to my astonishment,
he offered me chocolate!
I had suggested we leave some useful objects
in the cellar I discovered on the island,
but instead they plundered it of salmon
and replaced food with tobacco,
a Chinese pipe, a piece of Chinese silk
and 20 glass beads. They did add

a couple of kettles and knives, but still
I think the natives will consider the exchange
a hostile one, especially since they might
not know what to do with the tobacco.

Verily, the seaman knows winds,
the shepherd sheep.
I was scarcely an hour on the ship when
Master Khitrov and his party of 15
returned from their excursion in the long boat.
With great excitement he told us he'd come across
a small habitation of wood, and near the hut
was found a wooden basket
in which were shell fish, proving
"the inhabitants here used them for food."
He presented a stone, a hollow ball
of hard-burned clay,
a fox's tail, and a paddle from a canoe.
These trivial objects he treated like prized booty.
He had not been able to find a suitable harbor.
Surely, once I present Commander Bering
with my findings, he will agree
we must return tomorrow for water
and anti-scorbutic plants
not to mention the chance to complete
my work as resident scientist.

„Eastward ho!", 2015

DER BRILLENKORMORAN
von Mikael Vogel

Schwer-
Flüglig, unbeholfen, federleicht zu
Töten: aufzupflückendes Fleisch …
Vertrauensvoll sein Aufblick zu Vitus Bering als
Dessen Schiffbruch auch ihm die Entdeckung
einbrachte. Laut Steller
Der ihm als einziger Zoologe jemals lebend
begegnete
Machte ein Kormoran drei hungrige Männer satt

„Dodos", 2018

**Brillen-
kormoran**
Zeichnung
John G.
Keulemans,
1907

113

Gedichte über Vitus Bering

Russische Gedenkmedaille
250 Jahre Fahrt an die Küste Amerikas von
Vitus Jonassen Bering, 1741

ODE AN DEN RUSSISCHEN KOLUMBUS

von Mikhail Vasil'evich Lomonosov

С берегов вечерных на восток.
Я вижу умными очами:
Колумб Российский между лдами
Спешит и презирает рок.

„Poezija", Ode Elisabeth, Strophe 12, 1752

Vergeblich wehret die gestrenge
Natura die verbindend Gänge
von West nach Ost uns mit Gewalt.
Dies meine klugen Augen schauen:
Durchs Eis strebt ohne Todesgrauen
der russische Kolumbus bald.

UNERFORSCHTE KÜSTE
von Igor Gurevich

НЕОТКРЫТЫЙ БЕРЕГ

Туманом окутался берег,
притих, как нашкодивший кот,
в надежде, что старенький Беринг
его, бедолагу, найдет.

И встанет на рейде корабль,
обвиснут, пальнув паруса.
Притихнут прибрежные крабы
на четверть последних часа —

и вот уже в теплый песчаник
с последним натужным «и раз!»,
с веселой матросскою бранью
воткнется забортный баркас.

В ботфортах судьбы командарм
на берег туманный взойдет,
как маршал на новый плацдарм,
как странник на свой звездолет.

От собственной славы хмелея —
так могут одни короли —
еще ни о чем не жалея,
он радостно скажет: «Дошли!» …

Туманом окутался берег,

который никто не открыл.

А Витус Иванович Беринг

в тумане незримо проплыл.

„Stikhi“, 2015

ECCLESIASTES
by Jeremiah Webster

The barndoor skate
had a wingspan of five feet
but was unable to escape the synthetic
nets of North Atlantic fishermen
who threw them back dead as bycatch.
It wasn't difficult, those eyes
staring out with clandestine dimness,
the alien structure more aircraft
than animal.

Pelicans, rarely seen, are often hooked
by trolling boats, dragged
underwater for miles;
their slight bodies buoy to the surface
only as they arrive at port.

Sharks can do nothing
but succumb to the thick
chumming off Japanese shores, the swift
harvest of fins and teeth.
Once aboard, appendages hewn,
the body is kicked back into the ocean
for the long swimless dive downward.

Here is St. Peter,
Vitus Bering's sea vessel of 1741.
The chief mate admires
how suitable the fusiform body is for the sea
before slaughtering the last sea cow.

„After so many Fires", 2017

Bering wird auf die Awatscha-Insel gebracht.

VITUS BERING
von W. G. Sebald

Vier Männer brachten Bering, dem das Wasser
nach und nach bis in den Leib gestiegen war,
auf einem aus Stricken gefertigten Sitz an Land,
lehnten ihn im Schatten des Winds an einen Felsen
und machten ein Dach aus den Segeln
des Hl. Peter. Gehüllt in Mäntel, Pelze und Roben,
gelbfaltigen Gesichts, der Mund,
zahnlos, eine schwarze Ruine,
von Karbunkeln und Läusen am ganzen
Körper geplagt, besah sich der Kapitän,
voller Zufriedenheit im Angesicht des Todes,
die ersten Arbeiten zur Errichtung
eines Winterquartiers in den in die Dünen
gegrabenen Höhlen der Füchse.

Steller bringt Bering eine aus Tran
und Nasturtiumwurzeln gekochte Suppe,
die Bering jedoch, den Kopf
zur Seite bewegend, ausschlägt
mit einem Blinken der Augen.
Man solle ihn jetzt,
meint er, ruhig in den Sand
sinken lassen.

Die Zaunkönige
springen bereits auf ihm herum.
Selig seynd die Toten, erinnert sich
Steller. Am 8. Dezember binden sie
den Kapitän auf ein Brett
und schieben ihn in die Grube hinab.
Nicht wollest Du, Herr, übergeben
die Seele derer, die Dich bekennen,
den wilden Thieren. Am Tag des Gerichts
soll vielmehr für die Frommen ein Mahl
bereitet werden aus dem Herz des Leviathans.
Steller, indem er aufblickt, sieht
den graugrünen Widerschein des Ozeans,
den arktischen Wasserhimmel,
unter den Wolken. Ein Zeichen,
wie weit sie noch sind
vom festen Land.

„Nach der Natur", Gedicht XV, 1995

DER KOMMODORE
von Aleksandr Borisovich Kerdan

КОМАНДОР

Хоть сам от моря, кажется, далёк

И в лоции совсем не безупречен,

Но выше жизни почитал он долг

И непосильный груз взвалил на плечи,

Чтоб кто-нибудь другой дерзнул посметь

И выполнил великую задачу …

И потому бессильна даже смерть

Ему в вину поставить неудачи.

И нам ли осуждать теперь его,

Наветам стародавним слепо вторя?

Да, не открыл он в жизни ничего,

Но нам оставил Берингово море.

„Podrobnosti zhizni", 2015

Die Kommandeurinseln
Bering- und Kupferinsel, 54-56 °N 166-168°E

KAPITAN-KOMANDOR V. BERING
von Sergej Sokolov

Потребовалось значительное время, прежде чем
заслуги Беринга были полностью признаны.
Первым из путешественников, подтвердившим
точность исследований Беринга, стал
английский мореплаватель Джеймс Кук.
Именно он предложил дать имя Беринга
проливу между Чукоткой и Аляской.

В 1874 году представители Российско-
Американской компании поставили деревянный
крест примерно на том месте, где
предположительно должна была находиться
могила великого мореплавателя. Позднее
местные исследователи установили нынешний
памятник — два наложенных друг на друга
каменных прямоугольника, покрытые сверху
чугунной плитой. Надгробие венчает железный
крест высотой 3,5 м.

Капитан, капитан Витус Беринг,
Где же суша сквозь плотный туман?
Только что слева был дикий берег …
Кто его для России измерит?
А сейчас впереди – океан.

Значит, нет впереди перешейка.
Пуповины с Америкой нет.

Страшный холод … Жены душегрейка.
Мчит корабль вдоль берега змейкой…
Мёртвый Пётр не узнает ответ

Ты по роду да с виду датчанин,
А душою давно уж русак.
Ты, склоняясь над картой ночами,
Подавляя порывы отчаянья,
Шёл к открытьям на всех парусах.

Экспедиции первой так мало?
Приключений желала душа.
Снова море под парус позвало,
Брал „Святой Пётр" высь вал за валом,
Мча с валов, словно в бездну спеша.

Капитан-командор Беринг Витус,
Знал ли ты, где тебе будет крест?
Моряки похоронною свитой
Под скалою ветрами избитой
Тремя залпами отдали честь.

Волны с ветром шумят в вечном споре,
Воздух белый от множества крыл.
В Петербурге – семейное горе…

Мореход умирает на море
Иль на бреге, что первым открыл.

„Stikhi", 2012

POEM FOR VITUS BERING
by Mary L. Kienholz

Did you feel trepidation
When Peter the Great
In seventeen-twenty-five
And again in seventeen-forty
sent you exploring?

Wooden sailing ships,
their hulls and great white dorsal fins
Dutifully shaped by skilled shipbuilders
In Kamchatka's arctic climate,
Were raised to please Peter, the Emperor.
And you named a town for him:
Petropavlovsk-Kamchatski.
Or was that for your ship
Plus Chirikov's:
Saint Peter and Saint Paul?
On that cold peninsula,
Where Klyuchevskaya spewed
Her lava, and the earth
Shakes in warning.
As your ship's sails later
Shivered in the freezing wind,
Did Intuition warn
That you would be cast
On a nearby island
And never see
Your Jutland home again?

„Adventures in Poetry", 2010

124

LEGACY FOR VITUS BERING
by Elizabeth Bradfield

They've closed again the gap that you first sailed,
Russian sponsored Dane, so cousins on the
Diomedes
are in post Cold War touch. But you made the map
that made the border, sighting lands just guessed at
between Kamchatka and America's west coast.
And we
write history from what's put down officially, maps
and logbooks made and kept by the survivors
of your death, of your loss of ambition from years
line-toeing across the forehead of Siberia.
Finally you set sail for
glory – or not for but from whatever pushes
us beyond
our birth-spots. What pushes us away? I, too,
have left
for some spot unknown by any who claim me, for
place unhooked from kin and story. I've fled
the watched life of any hometown where if
you kick a dog, infect a girl, break a window
the girl turns out to be your mother's landlord's
cousin, the dog a beat cop's mutt, and shards
cut your sister's foot: Each chafed-at things
a window

in your glass-house world. So the age-old lust
for places
we pretend are free of consequence. It's the same
now as it was with Oedipus, poor stiff, running
to escape his fate
and running smack dab into it, an awful
scene, a nightmare warning we need to keep
repeating because, of course, fate
never seems immediate. For weeks Bering's crew
feasted
on the delicious bulk of sea cows (now extinct).
They played cards, anted up with otter pelts
that promyshlenniki later
stripped from the shores. Foxes bit the men's toes
at night. The land ate them as they ate the land,
calling it need, worrying about it later.

„Approaching Ice", 2010

Paketboot
Sv. Pavel mit
A. Chirikov,
1741.
Medaille 250
Jahre
Entdeckung
Russisch
Amerikas

VITUS BERING
by Earle Birney

Asia eastward cannot end
said the tsar's most loyal geographers.
But that Danish farmboy knew the sea
no less persistent than was he.

Picket bones of schooners in the Baltic mud
joined them in a Kamchatkan spring
launched a Gabriel with patchwork wings
untrumpeted into the sunrise,
into a nothingness of fog and gull-cries.
Fumbled north and bumped his packfloe sea
marked off Russia from infinity.

Tenacious as the sleet he weathered home
enlisted Chirikov, St. Paul, St. Peter
somewhere eastward lay that farthest west.
But the devil's fog divided the Apostles,
It was the Russian saw Alaskas's icy castles
while God's last and loneliest Norseman tacked
from the roaring ambush of the Aleutians back
bare-ribbed and scurvy-scarred
to the remotest islet he could give the tsar.
And patiently he froze there in a sandpit.

Dead as he were soon the bellowing seabulls
he created; the million sables
bled a little slower. To keep the massacre
exclusive, the tsar's most loyal geographers
affirmed that eastward Asia did not end.

„Candlemas", 1965

AMERICA
by Jennifer Dunbar Dorn

On June 26 the St. P*eter*
gave up the search for *St. Paul*
and the illusive Company Land.
Bering ordered a North East course
and retired to his cabin, where
the irony of his fate kept him awake
and he had nightmares in which
the men screamed for help
as the decks of *St. Paul* sank
and Alexei Chirikov went under.

In fact, Chirikov and his men,
having given up the search for *St. Peter*
were now heading northeast, too,
and would make several landings
along the coast of what is now Alaska,
but Bering would never know it.
What little hope he had left
left when he lost Chirikov.
Even Steller's company irritated him,

and he could see now why the men
called the young German arrogant.
Steller claimed he could sound depths
and smell land from miles away.
He said certain sea plants and birds
indicated land lay close by
and lectured on the habitat of creatures
playing around the boat —
he'd seen them in Kamchatka —
who never venture far from shore.
He acted like a child the way
he wanted to be the first
to set eyes on America.
The crew teased him mercilessly.
Fog and rain continued for 3 weeks.
They veered east northeast —
the water on board was half gone
when Steller again swore he saw land
although there was no bottom at 90 fathoms.
At 12:30 the next day, July 16,
the clouds lifted, revealing the Alaskan range
topped by Mt. St. Elias.
As the men filled the decks, cheering
Bering shrugged and
disappeared below.

Two days passed before
the weather was calm enough
to anchor off Kayak Island.
Khitrov who had lost the biscuits
went in a long boat
to find a safer harbor.
Steller, who was not allowed to go,

stormed around the deck
in disbelief and anger.
Bering appeared to enjoy this display
of sulking, treating it as a big joke,
and when he finally suggested
that Steller join the watering party,
he summoned the ship's trumpeters
and had everyone cheer
as Steller boarded the boat
and with his Cossack Thomas
and a small crew, headed for shore.
It was about 9 o'clock in the morning.
Steller was not sure,
when he looked back
whether Bering was smiling
or sneering at him.

„Eastward Ho!", 2015

**Portrait
von
Vitus Bering**
Rekonstruktions-
versuch der
Russischen
Akademie
der
Wissenschaften,
1991

DER KOPF DES VITUS BERING
von Konrad Bayer

theorie der schiffahrt

vitus bering hat reisen um die erde angestellt, und zwar zu schiffe, aber nirgends fand er ein ende oder eine kante.

des nachts sahen die seefahrer flämmchen wie sterne auf der meeresfläche, oft folgte dem schiffe ein feuriger schweif und bezeichnete den weg, welchen das schiff zurückgelegt hatte, oft auch schien das ganze meer in feuer zu stehen, so weit das auge reicht, und das schiff ging durch ein feuermeer

?

entsteht hiedurch tag und nacht?

also.

die erde ist ein körper und schwebt im raum. dabei dreht sich dieser körper um sich selbst. dazu braucht er zirka 24 stunden.

tag und nacht stand oder lag vitus bering in und auf einem schiff, dessen kommando er führte.

zeit

1728 war nicht die richtige zeit für bering. da wurde er 13 jahre älter und fuhr noch einmal mit einem gewissen steller, der dann auch die

stellersche seekuh entdeckte, die dann auch bis zu
8 meter lang wurde.

ausscheidung (auswahl)

in der tat sprang bering mehr, als er ging, den bug
hinan und schritt, stets das gesicht nach jener luke
am bugende gerichtet, elastisch und selbstbewußt
die reeling entlang.

erklärung (21. märz)

als bering die fische mit öl goss, nahm er damals
wieder platz und verzehrte damals alles.

der hut des vitus bering

ein filzhut aus biberhaar, breitkrempig.

freiheit und körperpflege

das lange haar war ein zeichen des freien mannes,
welches bering in einem zopf trug, der ihm her-
unterhing. bering besass eine puderdose und eine
brennschere aus silber. wenn er schlechter laune
war, besorgte er seine haare selbst, sonst rief er sei-
nen diener deschneff, nicht zu verwechseln mit
simon deschneff, vielmehr ein gewisser deschneff,

der den ruf eines hervorragenden haarkünstlers
genoss. als kommandeur eines schiffes hatte
bering alle verfügungsgewalt und war sein eigener
herr. vitus bering verurteilte einen gewissen
deschneff zu 15 stockhieben, weil er ihm die haare
verbrannt hatte. dennoch vermählte er niemand,
da damen fehlten.
sowohl in geographischer wie in naturhistorischer
hinsicht ist die beringinsel eine der merkwürdigsten
inseln im nördlichen teil des stillen ozeans.
hier war es,
wo bering als schiffbrüchiger seine
entdeckerlaufbahn
beschloss, er wurde von vielen seiner begleiter
überlebt, unter diesen von dem arzt und naturfor-
scher steller, welcher eine mit selten übertroffener
meisterschaft
ausgeführte schilderung der naturverhältnisse und
des tierlebens auf dieser früher nie von menschen
besuchten insel gegeben hat, auf der er die zeit von
november 1741 bis ende august 1742 zubringen
musste.
(die umsegelung asiens und europas auf der vega v.
adolf erik freiherr von nordenskiöld,
brockhaus 1882)

„Der Kopf des Vitus Bering", 2014

SOME REMARKS
by Jennifer Dunbar Dorn

Steller says that Bering
often regretted that his strength
was no longer sufficient
for so difficult an expedition.
"He expressed the desire
that on account of his age
he might be released from duty
and the task of commander assigned
to someone younger and more active."
Sokoloff says that Bering
was well informed,
eager for knowledge, pious,
kind-hearted and honest, but
altogether too cautious and indecisive;
zealous, persevering and yet
not sufficiently energetic;
well liked by his subordinates, but
without enough influence over them,
too much inclined by their opinions and desires
to maintain strict discipline.

Steller allows that Bering
was not naturally
a man of great resolve,

but doubts whether another
possessed of more fire and ardor
could have overcome the immense difficulties
of the expedition
without completely ruining
those distant regions.
Indeed, part of Bering's growing reluctance
to lead the expedition may have
come from knowing all too well
what follows in the wake
of such an invasion —
not just the army of men
but their diseases, not just
guns and vodka, but the hunter,
the greedy businessman, the rapist,
the yassack collector.

„Eastward ho!", 2015

**Vitus Bering
zu seinem
300-jährigen Geburtstag:
Vier-Kopeken-Briefmarke
der Post der UdSSR, 1981**

VITUS BERING UND SEINE ZWEI KAMTSCHATKA-EXPEDITIONEN

von Vladimir Tjaptin

ПОЭМА О ВИТУСЕ БЕРИНГЕ И ДВУХ ЕГО КАМЧАТСКИХ ЭКСПЕДИЦИЯХ

1 Вступление

Ай да Витус! Ай да Беринг!
Сколько он всего открыл!
Что ни море, что ни берег –
Всё он видел, всюду был.
В честь его названий столько
Территорий! – Подсчитать –
Больше, чем вмещает Волга,
Всюду можно отыскать. –
И пролив, и даже море,
Остров Беринга, где он
Зорко смотрит вечным взором
На далёкий горизонт.
Есть и мыс в его же море;
Рядом с озером ледник. –
«На Аляске?» – Да, на взморье
Можно там увидеть их.
Даже бывший перешеек

Беренгией назван, и
Он – посёлок, парк с аллеей,
Где резвятся малыши.
Он – и улицы в десятке
Городов и две – в Москве,
«Bering Air» на Аляске
И в российской синеве.
Ледокол буксирный назван;
Его имя – датский бренд
И часов моднейших; разве
Он не университет?» –
«И за что такая слава?
Как он этого достиг?» –
«Потрудился он на славу
И поэтому велик.

2 Первая Камчатская экспедиция (1725 – 1730)

Два похода на Камчатку
Героически свершил
И в обоих бил в десятку,
Много нового открыл.
Сам Пётр Первый перед смертью
Повелел направить вдаль
Экспедицию – проверить,
Есть пролив ли, приказал
Лично Берингу – построить
Два надёжных корабля,

Чтоб на них пошли герои,
На Америку руля.
Только вдумайтесь – два года
Добирался он в Охотск! –
Пеше, конно, вплавь. Дорогой
Столько мучиться пришлось!
Зимовать пришлось в Охотске,
А затем на лодках и
На упряжках, ветер в очи,
На собачьих вдаль пошли.
«Помнишь ли, река Камчатка,
Как добрались к устью здесь?»
Да, вот это, братцы, хватка!
Есть герои мире, есть!
На Камчатском побережье,
Там, где плещет океан,
Строят судно – ветер свежий
Мчит на север, как буян.
Три залива, бухта, остров
Здесь на карту внесены
И прошли пролив. Ну, просто,
Замечательные дни!
Вот герои так герои! –
Подтвердили: «Есть пролив!»
А раз так – само собою
В сердце – радостный мотив.
Обогнув Камчатку с юга,

Возвращаются в Охотск
И чрез всю Сибирь-подругу –
В Петербург пешком в поход.
Дан доклад, к нему – записки,
В них уверенность – близки
И Америка, и виски.
А раз так – вперёд, сынки!

3 Вторая Чукотская экспедиция (1733 – 1741)

От Тобольска до Якутска
Путь лежит теперь в их честь.
И три года здесь толкутся
Беринг с Чириковым здесь:
Ох, препон, препятствий много!
Наконец, они вдали –
Вновь в Охотске и три года
Строят там им корабли:
Рогачёв, Кузьмин отлично
С этим справились. Ура! –
На Камчатку – им привычно
Прокричать – пришла пора.
Хороша река Авача!
Бухта тоже хороша!
«Здесь зимуют?» – Не иначе,
Хоть и рвётся в путь душа.
Поселенье заложили –
Надо ж где-то зимовать?

Петропавловск здесь явили. —
«Эх, какая благодать!»
Отправляются навстречу
«С кем? С Америкою?» – «Да».
Шторм, туман. Ещё не вечер —
Зримость – только до борта.

Как ослепли – потеряли
В шторм друг друга корабли.
Поискали, поискали
И разрозненно пошли.

И к Америке подходят
«Павел», следом «Пётр». Вот так
На день «Пётр отстал». – «Выходит,
Он вторым пришёл?» – «Да», так.

И, решив, что прогуляться
По Америке пора,
Сходят на берег. Аляска
Их встречает под «Ура!»

«Эх, Каяк, тебя бы надо
Здесь, на этом рубеже
Сделать Берингом, но надо ль,
Если имя есть уже?»

Погуляли, отдохнули,
Поглядели на гору,
На прощание кивнули
И вернулись к кораблю.

И теперь идут обратно

Без соседа за бортом.
Что поделаешь? Отрадно
Было б плыть назад рядком.
Вдоль Аляски и дугою
Алеутских берегов
«Пётр» плывёт и пред собою
Видит много островов.
Беринг всех берёт на карту:
«Эх, открытий сколько вновь!»
Хорошо вот так с азартом
Плыть до новых берегов.
Но всему конец приходит.
Новый остров на пути. –
Это кстати. В бухту входят –
Надо им набрать воды.
Ах, ты, мать честная! – Ветер
Бросил на берег корабль.
Ох, уж, вечно штучки эти! –
Сломан! Надо зимовать!
И цинга напала – косит
Уж команду, как коса.
Да и Беринг под вопросом –
Заболел, закрыл глаза.
И скончался». – «Как скончался?» –
«Да, восьмого декабря.
И на острове остался». –
«Погребён был здесь он?» – «Да». –

«А с командой что случилось?
Не погибли ли они?» –
«Те, кто выжил, отличились» –
С наступлением весны
Из обломков, надо ж, ух ты!
Гукор собран ими был
И в Авачинскую бухту
Вместе с ними он приплыл.

4 Заключение

Так закончились походы
По земле и по воде
Мореплавателя. Вроде,
Нет его, и он везде:
Он живёт на картах мира,
Каждый в мире человек
Его знает, честь мундира,
Слава мчат из века в век.
Слава мчат из века в век.
Вот такой герой России –
Хоть датчанином рождён,
Ей отдал все свои силы,
В ней Отечество обрёл.

„Stikhi“, 2018

BERINGS BEGRÄBNIS
von Andrej Bronnikov

Корабль выброшен на скалы незнакомого
острова.

Полкоманды больны. Командор умирает.
Прозрачный ручей утоляет жажду. Люди роют
землянки, спасаясь от холода. Плоский берег
незаметно сменяется морем. Много животных.
Они не боятся нас. Ветер гонит тучи. Никого.
Этот остров необитаем. Казак тащит по песку
тушу калана. У нас есть пропитанье. Переждать
до весны.

Переждать зиму здесь и плыть потом дальше.
До берега сотни миль если верить положению
солнца.

Крики чаек напоминают о чем-то давнем.
Надо заняться гербарием. На любом из таких
островов

поджидает сюрприз. Новый цветок, неизвестная
птица,

тюлень или мышь. Командор умер тихо, во сне.
Похоронен отдельно, привязан к доске.
Этот остров теперь навсегда связан с ним.
Из обломков палубы сделан надежный крест.
В ясный день виден с моря. Покорные волны,
как барашки, бегут вдали Дай им знак, командор

Было время – водили они тобой, теперь – ты
пастырь их.

„Исчезающий Вид", *2008/2009*

BERINGS BEGRÄBNIS
von A. Bronnikov, übersetzt von Christine Hengevoß

Das Schiff, geworfen auf die Klippen einer
unbekannten Insel.
Die halbe Mannschaft krank. Der Kommandeur
im Sterben.
Den Durst stillt eine klare Quelle. Die Leute
schaufeln
Erdhütten, als Schutz vor der Kälte.
Der flache Strand
wird zum Meer, unmerklich fast. Hier gibt es
viel Getier.
Zahm sind die Tiere, ohne Angst. Wolken im
Wind. Kein Mensch außer uns.
Eine unbewohnte Insel. Einer der Kosaken schleift
einen toten Seeotter
durch den Sand. Nahrung ist also vorhanden.
Warten bis zum Frühjahr.
Überwintern und dann weiterfahren.
Glaubt man der Stellung der Sonne, sind es
Hunderte von Meilen bis zur Küste.
Die Möwenschreie lassen an Fernes, Vergangenes
denken.
Ich muss am Herbarium arbeiten. Jede dieser
Inseln

wartet mit einer Überraschung auf. Eine neue
Blume, ein unbekannter Vogel,
eine Robbe, eine Maus. Der Kommandeur ist im
Schlaf, ganz still
gestorben. Wir begruben ihn für sich, gebunden
an eine Planke.
Nun ist die Insel mit ihm für immer verbunden.
Aus Bruchstücken des Mastes haben wir ein
haltbares Kreuz gefertigt.
Bei klarer Sicht ist es vom Meer zu sehen.
In der Ferne laufen,
wie Schäfchen, ergebene Wellen. Gib ihnen ein
Zeichen, Kommandeur!
Einst führten sie dich. Jetzt bist du ihr Hirte.

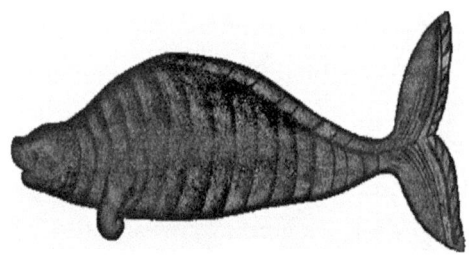

LE OSSA DI BERING
von Andrea Gibellini

Ghiaccio e non altro se ghiaccio disteso,
il biancore della marea e il vento, sua meraviglia
feroce.
– Che tutto, ora, si annienti, apertamente.

Si staccano leggere, defogliano semispente, perenni
come in una stagione orribilmente sognata.
Scuro leone marino, tiepido giorno …

„Le ossa di Bering", 1993

BERING'S BONES
von Andrea Gibellini, übersetzt von N.S. Thompson

Ice, nothing but stretches of ice,
the pallor of the sea and fierce wonder of the wind.
– Everything negated now, plainly.

Detached delicately, they fall like half-dead leaves,
eternal in this dreadful nightmare season.
A dark sea lion, a lukewarm day…

„The Copenhagen Review", 2018

BERINGS GEBEINE
von Andrea Gibellini, übersetzt von Harald Pinl

Eis und nichts anderes als Eisfelder,
Fahlheit der Gezeiten und der Wind,
wunderlich heftig.
– Alles ist nun zu nichte, offensichtlich.

Leicht abgelöst, wie halbverweste Überbleibsel,
auf ewig in einer Zeit schrecklichen Albtraumes.
Ein dunkler Seelöwe, ein kühler Tag …

250 Jahre seit der Entdeckung Russisch Amerikas
Kapitan-Komandor V. Bering mit dem Paketboot
„Svjatoj Petr", 1741
25-Rubel-Münze aus der Historischen Serie der
UdSSR, 1990

Gedichte über Kamtschatka
und die Kommandeur-Inseln

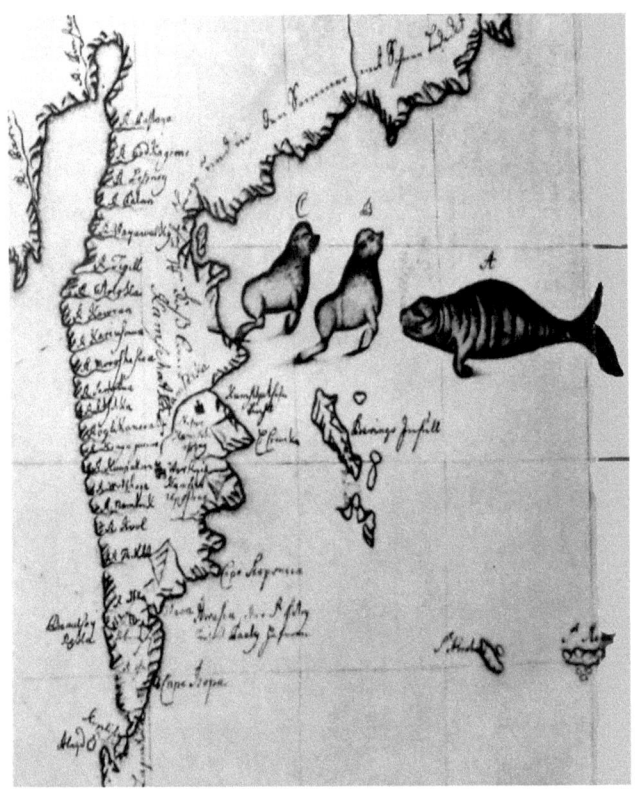

Aus der Kamtschatka-Skizze von Sven Waxell, 1742
A Seekuh, B Seelöwe, C Seebär

KAMCHATKA
by Roald Hoffmann

From Vietnam era helicopters
you first see "smoke". Closer,
the lakes and broken rim
of Uzon caldera paint in steam
a Monet land, blues and yellows,
Up close, pool upon pool, crystal
clear, one on the way to orange,
bubbles plopping threateningly
through the mud clay of another.

And life, in every shade but green.
For this isn't the photosynthetic
world – my silver rings turn black
from hydrogen sulfide. Water
bubbles up boiling at 95°C; pH
paper makes out that water acid
as nitric, elsewhere drain-cleaner
basic; I'd not touch it cool. Round
each pool, life – dull red, yellow,
beige mats of bacteria, archaea.

Eight months of the year, Uzon
caldera is under snow. Water,
seeping down to the magma
is shot up, in percolating flow

depositing, dissolving. This is
geochemistry in the fast forward
mode – here realgar, pyrite,
five meters down maybe gold.

Some like it hot. Some want O2,
some do not. This niche came,
the rest – evolution's game
tinker; give it time, hazard, and.
from C, N, H, O, S, metals, life
finds its way; those mats – in
a hell of acid and heat (to us) –
find a dear place to play, and
pry survival out a few genes.
Pyrolobus fumarii grows best
at one hundred and thirteen°C.

It's not done with mirrors, but
in watery molecular stratagems.
Eggs (protein too), would cook,
cell walls melt in Uzon's pools.
Hyperthermophiles, the same
and not the same, in their walls
an ether linkage brace, proteins
made tough by straight runs of
resistant amino acids, and DNA,
finds bodyguards in polyamines,

basic proteins, reverse gyrases,
and a really good repair shop.

So they adapt, like the folk
who live here, who serviced
the submarines of the old
USSR, and now that the ships
rust and midwinter electricity
is on but three hours a day,
they are still here, sell berries
and black radishes at market,
drive stolen Japanese cars,
eat fish at every meal, drink.
They are here, at the periphery,
nine hours flight from Moscow,
where eagles feed their young,
the earth trembles, bears pace
the streams when salmon run.

And some of us are fishers
of archaea, if not of men
or salmon; will you eat sulfur,
or hydrogen, or iron salts; we,
so smart, would know how ---
there's acid, heat, dazzle us
oh organism with your holistic
web of tricks! And some of us

are newfangled fishers ---
for DNA, for isn't it all, all
that matters? That makes you
puffer fish or mouse, inscribes
in a four letter code blueprints
for every inner assembly line?
Who knows, the hot spring's dirt
might hide a billion dollar gene.
And what will Kamchatka get?

On a piece of walrus scrimshaw,
a well-dressed Russian bear
rests on a sled. He's tired, like
our students after a long day's
collecting, who now sit cross-
legged on the floor, stabilizing
their DNA. The bear holds
in his hands a steaming cup,
there's a kettle on the snow.
Somewhere there must be a fire;
behind him a smoking volcano.
Kamchatka, bearing sweet life.

„Mosty", 2014

KAMCHATKA!
by Liz Poey

Kamchatka!
Kamchatka!
Land of snow, wind, wilderness
And volcanoes
Kamchatka!
Home of reindeers, brown bears
And hardy Even people
Kamchatka!
Destination of clueless city folks
And dreamers
Kamchatka!
Hidden, untouched, untrodden
A lost world ... found.

„The Lost World guest's book", 2012

**Hafen von Sankt Peter und Paul in Stellers
„Beschreibung von dem Lande Kamtschatka"**

KAMTSCHATKA!

von Liz Poey, übersetzt von Joachim Ruf

Kamtschatka!
Land aus Schnee, Wind, Wildnis
Und Vulkanen
Kamtschatka!
Heimat von Rentieren, Braunbären
Und kühnem Evenen-Volk
Kamtschatka!
Ziel von ahnungslosen Stadtmenschen
Und Träumern
Kamtschatka!
Versteckt, unberührt, unbetreten.
Eine verlorene Welt … gefunden.

**Der feuerspeiende Berg Kamtschatka aus
Stellers „Beschreibung vom Lande Kamtschatka"**

HALBINSEL KAMTSCHATKA
von Vladimir Tataurov

ПОЛУОСТРОВ КАМЧАТКА. 1720-1730 гг.

Спит за речкой атынум.
Лишь в берёзах ветра шум,
Да собаки завывают.
У костра шаман камлает:

«Лельга, онъга, эхамчи!
Ричи чичи чичичи!
Лени нули эли ами!
Бичикако никако… ».

Путешествует шаман
По далёким временам.
«Гушъ-гушъ …
Хай-хай …
Ишки-Ишки !!! » –
По чужим мечтам и снам.
Непонятные дела –
Тени, руки и тела …
И внезапно – лица, лица.
И опять в который раз –
Та же девочка без глаз.
И кричат:
«Квас-ник Го-ли-цын!»

Чей-то плач и чей-то стон …
Средь Анфис, Елен, Матрон
Прячется шамана дочка.

Выстрел.

Словно в сердце – кол!
Разом стало так легко.
«Бу-же-ни-но-ва Ав-до-тья-я-я …»

2

Шли для сбора ясака
Два якутских казака
Злыдень Федька и Иван.
Смотрят сквозь кусты:
Шаман
У костра хрипит в ночи:
«Лельга, онъга, эхамчи …».

Федька взял ружьё Ивана.
Был шаман –
И нет шамана.

В тимусчичь через жупан
С факелом вошёл Иван.
В куче рухляди гнилой
Кто-то прячется живой.
Федька – прыг.

И, как рыбёшку,
Вытащил на свет ребёнка.

«Я – палач!
Закон!
И суд!
Всех убью!
Не то убьют
Нас ватаги ительменов,
И коряков, и эвенов …
Мало нас.
Не долог срок,
Не спасёт от них острог.
Ванька, раздевай ребёнка!
Кто там? –
мальчик
аль девчонка?
Мальчик – враг!
Его убьём!
Девочку с собой возьмём».

Не спеша разобрались.
От греха убереглись.
«Ну, живи тогда, зверёныш!».
Улыбается детёныш.
Ай, забавная мордашка!
Зубы, словно у евражки.

3

Вот ясачная казна
Снова доверху полна.
Будет долгою дорога:
Ламским морем переход
На «Фортуне» на Охотск
С Большерецкого острога,
На Якутск и на Тобольск.
Казаки берут с собой
Дуньку со смешной мордашкой.
Шибко девка весела
И вертлява, как юла.
Зубы, словно у евражки,
Не дают закрыть ей рот.
Пусть потешится народ.
Будет в трудный час подругой.
Грузят в трюмы казаки
С мягкой рухлядью тюки.
Добрый путь до Петербурга!

„Vosmoj stolp Rossii", 2018

THE BERING BRIDGE
by Roald Hoffmann

The old men say
the sky was once so close
that if you shot an arrow up
it would bounce back at you. The sky
swallowed birds. Sometimes it lay
like the luxuriating fog
just above our tents
and a man could climb
to the opening at the top, where the smoke
went out
and talk to the gods.
Then the redwoods came, sacrificing
all to the main trunk, and
they jacked up the sky,
and then men with balloons and telescopes
pushed it back further,
so it became difficult to talk straight to the gods,
one had to yell, or use the intercession of shamans.
Now I have flown myself across the Pacific,
seen the deep sky blue at 30,000 ft.
They say a man has walked on the moon. They
say the earth is getting warmer.
I see smog, the sky coming back down over
California.

„Memory Effects", 1999

DIE ENTDECKER
von Aleksandr Borisovich Kerdan

ПЕРВОПРОХОДЦЫ

Анатолию Омельчуку

Через прихожую Сибири
Рванули смело на восток:
Своё ещё не долюбили
Уже в чужом познали толк.
Чтоб жилы рвать, вгрызаясь в жилы
Заморского материка,
Не ради призрачной наживы
След оставляли на века
На скалах сумрачной Аляски,
В могучих брёвнах форта Росс,
Чтоб сочинять об этом сказки
Потомкам дальним довелось …
Чтоб прорастала русским словом
Американская земля,
Россия вновь шагнуть готова
От стен Тобольского кремля.

„Podrobnosti zhizni", 2015

GAMALAND
by Jennifer Dunbar Dorn

On May 24, 1741, the *St. Peter*, commanded by
Vitus Bering, with a crew of 77,
and the *St. Paul*, commanded by Alexei Chirikov,
with a crew of 76, weighed anchor.
Then suddenly the wind dropped —
even at the point of departure they were
stopped, and the ships stood like
trees in the mouth of the bay.
Almost 2 weeks passed
before they again hoisted sail.
With Chirikov ahead and the men cheering
on June 4 they headed out of Avacha Bay
and set course for Gamaland,
the mythical island on Delisle's map.
De la Croyère insisted upon it.
The professor with his instruments and supplies
accompanied Chirikov.
Relieved to be at sea, Bering
hardly felt elated.
Having dragged an expedition
the size of a small army
across Siberia and Kamchatka,
he had orders to go south east
in search of what some charts called

Company Land, which was prophetic
since this voyage paved the way
for the future Russian-American Fur Company.
Bering knew nothing was there
but still, he followed instructions,
charted everything, even empty seas.
He took on the resigned air of
a man drowning in his own fate,
who'd gone too far to turn back,
whose hair had grown white.

"Eastward Ho!", 2015

Das mystische „Gamaland",
die angeblich von João da Gama entdeckten Inseln auf einer
Karte von Teixeira Albernez, 1643

AUF ALASKA
von Aleksandr Borisovich Kerdan

НА АЛЯСКЕ

Горбятся тотемы рода Ворона,
Над покатой крышею жилья.
Стайки звёзд шарахаются в стороны,
Словно испугавшись воронья.

Мхом поросший лес хранит молчание
О давнишнем споре – кто кого …
Об открытьях, сделанных датчанином,
А вернее, вовсе без него.

О простых, с мужицкою ухваткою,
Людях, что пришли издалека,
Распрощавшись с Курском, Тотьмой, Вяткою,
Да вот здесь оставшись на века –

В золоте крестов на колоколенках,
В именах, что носят острова –
Русским духом, самой малой толикой,
Что ещё в Америке жива.

Горькая, уже не знаменитая,
Но родная – тем и дорога –
Наша кровь, как ветвь, к дичку привитая,
Превратила в родича врага.

И недаром эту память жгучую
Чёрный ворон стережёт сейчас
Словно сон, что радует и мучает,
И к легенде приобщает нас.

Verfasst 2010. „Podrobnosti zhizni", 2015

GERASSIM PRIBILOV AND SAINT PAUL ISLAND

by Mary Lilly Kienholz

In 1786, sea otters, seals,
And high adventure lured
Gerassim Pribilov,
As they had Chirikov
And Vitus Bering.

It would seem
That paddling in the Bering Sea
In lesser boats
To locate breeding grounds
Of fur seals

Would not lure too many men.
Still, how fantastic
Were the seal rookeries of pushy bulls,
Females and their pups.
Slippery as fish!

They reclined on the rocks
In May migration.

The nearby cliffs
Animated with sea birds.
As numerous as bits of paper
Blown from an origami artist's desk.
Cormorants, puffins, gulls.

Such a payoff

For a dangerous trek.

Is it surprising
That these fur seal islands
Are called the Pribilovs?
That this isle's name,
Saint Paul, recalls
A Jutland searcher's ship.
From another time?

„Adventures in Poetry", 2010

Joachim Ruf und Mikhail Chirikov
vor der Bering-Statue auf der Beringinsel, 2016

Nachwort

Alexander Puschkin über Kamtschatka, Krascheninnikow und Steller

von Vladimir A. Abashnik

Im Mittelpunkt dieses Beitrags steht ein bis jetzt wenig beachteter Aspekt der literarischen Tätigkeit von Alexander Sergejewitsch Puschkin (1799–1837), nämlich dessen Beschäftigung mit der Kamtschatkageschichte. Zuerst wird hier auf die späteren historischen Arbeiten von Puschkin am Ende von 1836 bzw. zu Beginn von 1837 eingegangen. Im zweiten Teil wird die Skizze der „Kamtschatka-Arbeit" (1837) von Puschkin dargestellt, der sie auf Grund der zweibändigen Abhandlung „Beschreibung des Landes Kamtschatka" (1755) von Stepan Petrowitsch Krascheninnikow (Krasheninnikov) (1711–1755) verfasst hatte. Im dritten Teil werden Puschkins Bezüge auf die Arbeiten von Stepan Krascheninnikow und Georg Wilhelm Steller (1709–1746) berücksichtigt.

Am 27. Januar 1837 (bzw. 8. Februar nach dem gregorianischen Kalender) wurde Alexander Puschkin im Duell tödlich verletzt, an dessen Folgen er zwei Tage später, also am 29. Januar 1837 (10.02.1837), in Sankt Petersburg starb. Etwa am 20.01.1837, also eine Woche vor der tödlichen Verletzung begann Puschkin an einer Abhandlung zu arbeiten. In der Puschkin-Forschung ist sie bekannt als Kamtschatka-Arbeit, -Angelegenheiten, -Entwurf bzw. -Skizze. Im 10. Band (1938) der Gesamtausgabe der Werke von A. S. Puschkin wurde sie als „Bemerkungen über Kamtschatka" veröffentlicht.

Wie bekannt, beschäftigte sich Puschkin am Anfang der 1830er Jahre mit der Geschichte des Zaren Peter I. Bis zum Ende 1836 hat er Materialien in verschiedenen Archiven zu diesem Thema gesammelt, um sein Werk 1837 bzw. 1838 zu publizieren. Es ist anzunehmen, dass Puschkins Kamtschatka-Studien im Kontext seiner Arbeiten an dem geplanten Werk zur „Geschichte des Peter I." waren. Als Grundlage für Puschkins Kamtschatka-Studien diente das zweibändige Werk „Beschreibung des Landes Kamtschatka" von Stepan Krascheninnikow, der sich hier auf verschiedene Arbeiten und Manuskripte von Georg Wilhelm Steller stützte. Wie bekannt, erschien die genannte Arbeit Krascheninnikows zum ersten Mal im Jahre 1755 sowie dann in der zweiten Aufl. im Jahre 1786. Am Anfang des 19. Jh.s wurde sie noch in der Reihe „Gesamte Ausgabe der gelehrten Reisen durch Russland" durch die Kaiserl. Akademie der Wissenschaften" (1818–19) herausgegeben. In Puschkins Bibliothek gab es die zweite Auflage dieses zweibändigen Werkes (Sankt Petersburg 1786).

Etwa im Januar 1837 begann Puschkin das genannte Werk zu lesen und daraus einige Auszüge zu machen. So entstand ein Entwurf, den Puschkin als die „Kamtschatka-Angelegenheiten, den 20. Januar 1837" mit eigener Hand beschriftet hat. Die genannte Kamtschatka-Skizze von Alexander Puschkin enthielt: 1) einen Plan seiner künftigen Arbeit; 2) die Notizen über die Eroberung von Kamtschatka; 3) einen vorläufigen Entwurf unter dem Titel „Die Kamtschatka-Angelegenheiten". Diese Arbeit plante Puschkin in dem ersten bzw. zweiten Heft der von ihm herausgegeben Zeitschrift „Zeitgenosse" (russ. Sovremennik) zu veröffentlichen. Im ersten und zweiten Punkt seiner Kamtschatka-Skizze bezog sich Puschkin mehrmals auf die „Beschreibung des Landes Kamtschatka" von Stepan Krascheninnikow. In diesem Kontext berücksichtigte Puschkin auch Georg Wilhelm Steller, indem er in dem Paragraphen „über den Kamtschatka-Krieg" auch den Punkt „Steller über die Fehde der Kamtschadalen" erwähnte.

Besonders ist hervorzuheben, dass Puschkin nach diesem Kamtschatka-Entwurf nichts mehr geschrieben hat. Somit wurde die ganze literarische Tätigkeit des russischen Dichters mit dem Kamtschatka-Thema sowie mit Krascheninnikow und Steller beendet.

Ausschnitt aus der
„Karte von der Lage von Kamtschatka", 1774

Quellenverzeichnis

Abashnik, Vladimir A.: Alexander Puschkin über Kamtschatka, Krascheninnikow und Steller. Autor an Joachim Ruf (2018-11-08)

Barker, Brian: Vanishing Acts – Poems. Southern Illinois University Press, 2019 (Crab Orchard Series in Poetry)

Bayer, Konrad: Der Kopf des Vitus Bering – Romanmontage. Salzburg : Jung und Jung, 2014, S. 31, 40 (Cotta's Bibliothek der Moderne)

Bennett, Doraine: Readers Theater for Global Explorers. Exeter (UK) : Libraries Unlimited, 2011 und in: Ditty of the Month Club (DMC), May 2016. URL: michellehbarnes.blogspot.com (2019-04-15). Die Gedichte sind während eines „Working manuscript poems based on Bering's Kamchatka expedition" entstanden.

Bierds, Linda: Roget's Illusion. Putnam 2014.
Dies.: Georg Steller – The American Expedition, 1742, in: The Journal – a literary magazine, 37.1, Winter 2013

Birney, Earle: Vitus Bering. In: Candlemas – A Quarterly of New Verse, 13 (1965), S. 8; auch in: The Thamarack Review.

Bradfield, Elizabeth: Approaching Ice – Poems. Persea Books, 2010

Bronnikov, Andrej: Исчезающий Вид – Species Evanescens [Ischezajushchij Vid – Schwindende Arten]. 2008/2009, S. 28-30, 51, 56-57

Chang, Jennifer: Slept – Poems. Poem Hunter 2014. URL: www.poemhunter.com (2019-04-14); vgl. auch in:

The History of Anonymity. The University of Georgia Press, 2008

Clark, Tom: mild, in: Empire of Skin. Santa : Rosa, Black Sparrow Press, 1997, S. 18

Davie, Donald: Collected Poems. Carcanet Press, 2002, S. 239

Day, David: Nevermore : A Book of Hours – Meditations on Extinction. Toronto : Quattro Books, 2012 (Fourfront Editions Quattro Poetry)

Detering, Heinrich: Old Glory – Gedichte. Göttingen : Wallstein, 2012, S. 24

Donnelly, Timothy: Hymn to Life – Poetry. North Amherst : Factory Hollow Press, 2014 und in: Magazine "Poetry", July/August 2014. Chicago : Poetry Foundation, 2014. Außerdem in: "The Problem of the Many". Seattle : Wave Books, 2019

Dunbar Dorn, Jennifer: Eastward Ho! – The Saga of Vitus Bering. New York 2015, S. 23-28, 31-35, 50-51

Fama: Steller's Sea Cow speaks. In: Extinction Poems from South Camden Community School Students (12.03.2011). Camden : Wordpress, 2011. URL: feral-theatre.wordpress.com (2019-04-15)

George, Richard: Poems. Poem Hunter, 2005. URL: www.poemhunter.com (2019-04-14)

Gibellini, Andrea: Le ossa di Bering – poeti di clan Destino. Forli : Nuova Compagnia Ditrice, 1993 und Bering's Bones, in: English Anthology, Faber Edition. The Copenhagen Review, 2018

Glenday, John: Grain. Basingstoke : Picador (Macmillan Publishers), 2009

Gurevich, Igor: Неоткрытый берег [Unerforschte Küste], in: Stikhi, 13.12.2015. URL: stihi.ru (2019-04-14)

Hass, Robert: Songs to Survive the Summer. In: Praise. New York : The Ecco Press, 1979, S. 48-68

Hoffmann, Roald: Memory Effects – Collection of Poems. Chicago : Calhoun Press, 1999, S. 62; Journal Mosty 42 (2014) S. 319-321.-Erscheint in Frankfurt a.M.

Kaufman, Wallace: Sic Vita – The life and work of an independent Thinker and an innovating doer. URL: Sicvita.com (2019-05-06)

Kerdan, Aleksandr Borisovich: Podrobnosti zhizni – Stikhotvorenija, poemi, perevody. Ekaterinburg : Izdat AsPUr, 2015

Kienholz, Mary Lilly: Adventures in Poetry – A Septenary Collection of Fascinating Poems for All Ages. iUniverse, 14.07.2010

Klee, Detlev Wilhelm: Lux autumnalis (26.08.2016). URL: www.luxautumnalis.de/die-seekuh (2019-04-13)

Lewis, J. Patrick: Swan Song – Poems of Extinction. Holzschnitte von Christopher Wormell. Mankato : Creative Editions, 2003, S. 10

Lomonosov, Mikhail Vasil'evich: Polnoe Sobranie Sochinenij [Gesammelte Werke]. Tom 8: Poezija,… Moskau-Leningrad, 1959, S. 307

Macari, Anne Marie: She Heads into the Wilderness. Autumn House Press, 2008

Mickelson, Jory: Evening, in: „Plenitude – Your queer literary magazine" 25.06.2018. Vgl. auch in: „Stirring – Internet-Journal". URL: stirringlit.com (2019-04-13)

Osherow, Jacqueline: The Hoopoe's Crown – Poems. BOA Editions, 2005

Poey, Liz: The Lost World guest's book, #404. Dankadresse vom 12.06.2012 in URL: www.travelkamchatka. com/guestbook (2019-05-03)

Schwartz, Jeremy: Ode to a Steller's Jay, in: Medium`s Daily Digest, 10.07.2017. URL: medium.com (2019-04-13)

Sebald, Winfried Georg: Nach der Natur. Elementargedicht. Frankfurt : Fischer, 1995; Berlin : Carl Hanser, 2015

Sexton, Tom: For the Sake of the Light – New and Selected Poems. Fairbanks : University of Alaska Press, 2009, S. 31-32

Sikelianos, Eleni: Make Yourself Happy. Minneapolis, MN : Coffee House Press, 2017

Sokolov, Sergej: Kapitan-komandoru Vitusu Beringu. In: Stikhi, 2012. URL: stihi.ru (2019-04-06)

Steller, Georg Wilhelm: Beschreibung von dem Lande Kamtschatka, dessen Einwohnern, deren Sitten, Nahmen, Lebensart und verschiedenen Gewohnheiten. Herausgegeben von J.B. Scherer. Frankfurt; Leipzig : Fleischer, 1774, S. 266
Ders.: G.. Stellers ausführliche Beschreibung von sonderbaren Meerthieren. Halle : Kümmel, 1753
Ders.: De bestiis marinis. In: Novi commentarii Ac.Sc.Imp. Petropolitanae, Tom II. Petroploi 1751, S. 289-398

Stolen, Joanne: Summit Outside – Steller's Jay. In: Summit Daily News (2011-02-19).
URL: www.summitdaily.com/news

Tataurov, Vladimir: Poluostrov Kamchatka 1720-1730 [Halbinsel Kamtschatka]. In: Vosmoj stolp Rossii – Poema [Die achte Stütze Russlands – Gedichte], in: Nevskij Al'manakh No. 5/2018

Tjaptin, Vladimir: Poema o Vituse Beringe. In: Stikhi, 2018. URL: stihi.ru/2018/12/23/2160

Webster, Jeremiah: Ecclesiastes. In: After so Many Fires. Anchor & Plume, 2017

Vogel, Mikael: Dodos auf der Flucht – Requiem für ein verlorenes Bestiarium. Berlin : Verlagshaus Berlin, 2018, S. 45, 47

Zuzga, Jason: Extinction Narrative. In: Heat Wake – Poems. Hanover, London : University Press of New England, 2016, S. 17 (Saturnalia Books)

Nachweis der Abbildungen

Vs   Kollage aus einer Kamtschatka-Skizze von Sven Waxell 1742 mit einer Stellerschen Seekuh und Vulkan-Silhouetten. Marinearchiv RGAVMF, St. Petersburg, Rukop. No 2/39, S. 70/71.

Rs   Steller-Skulptur in Bronze, 70 cm hoch, von Il'ja
012   Pavlovich V'juev, Moskau 2016. Photo von Inna Aleksandrovna Lipilina in: Windsheimer Zeitung (Nürnberger Nachrichten)/Stefan Blank (2017-11-27) S. L 01; vgl. auch Skulpturnaja galereja „Geroj Russkoj Amerikii" von Il'ja V'juev unter URL: nic.pnb.ru/istorija-otechestva (2019-04-22)

067   Skelett einer Stellerschen Seekuh von der Seite,
      im Naturhitorischen Museum in Wien. Photo
      Harald Pinl, März 2018. Mit freundlicher Ge-
      nehmigung des NHM Wien.

068   Größenvergleich Mensch – Seekuh. Nach An-
      ders Jahan Retzius 1794 und Prehistoric Wildlife,
      URL: www.prehistoric-wildlife.com (2019-04-16)

071   Vulkane auf Kamtschatka. Titelbild zu Stellers
      "Beschreibung vom Lande Kamtschatka", 1774

075   Skelett einer Stellerschen Seekuh von vorn, im
      Naturhitorischen Museum in Wien.
      Photo Harald Pinl, März 2018. Mit freundlicher
      Genehmigung des NHM Wien.

083   „Pekarskische Abbildung": RGAVMF (Russlän-
      disches Staatliches Archiv der Seekriegsflotte), St.
      Petersburg. Vgl. auch Rothauscher, Hans: Die
      Stellersche Seekuh. Norderstedt : BoD, 2011, S.
      65 und Wikimedia.org/Commons (2019-02-08)

085   Stellers „Sonderbare Meerthiere" in: G.W. Stel-
      lers ausführliche Beschreibung von sonderbaren
      Meerthieren. Halle : Kümmel, 1753, S. 219;
      „Meerotter an Land und im Wasser". De bestiis
      marinis, in: Novi Commentarii Akademiae Scien-
      tiarum Imp. Petropolitanae – Tom. II, Petropoli
      1751, Tab. XVI

088   Steller vermisst eine Seekuh. Zeichnung von
      Leonhard Hess Stejneger: Steller's Journal of the
      Sea Voyage from Kamchatka to America. 1925,
      S. 228. Vgl. Wikipedia Commons (2019-04-30)

090   Pelztierjagd auf der Insel St. Paul: Chasse aux
      otaries. Holzstich 1880-1890, nach einem Photo

URL: www.scheideanstalt.de (2019-04-16)

Verzeichnis der Dichter*innen und Übersetzer*innen

Verzeichnis der Gedichte
und ihrer Anfänge

Hinweis:
Wer sich über die Gedichte hinaus mit den angesprochenen Themen beschäftigen möchte, dem sei die Steller-Gesellschaft in Halle empfohlen, u.a. mit ihrem Internetauftritt unter: www.steller-gesellschaft.de